HI, I'D LIKE TO GIVE YOU A FREE GIFT

Peter Duncan Whitford

WESTBOW
PRESS®
A DIVISION OF THOMAS NELSON
& ZONDERVAN

WestBow Press books may be ordered through booksellers or by contacting:

WestBow Press
A Division of Thomas Nelson & Zondervan
1663 Liberty Drive
Bloomington, IN 47403
www.westbowpress.com
1 (866) 928-1240

ISBN: 978-1-9736-8500-5 (sc)
ISBN: 978-1-9736-8502-9 (hc)
ISBN: 978-1-9736-8501-2 (e)

Library of Congress Control Number: 2020902249

Print information available on the last page.

WestBow Press rev. date: 06/23/2020

This book is dedicated to everyone who cares about the lost, the unsaved—those who don't know Jesus Christ as their Lord and Savior—and are committed to doing something about it by going out and sharing the Good News of Jesus Christ.

CONTENTS

Part 2 - My Journal

ACKNOWLEDGMENTS

I want to thank and acknowledge the extremely valuable help of Adele, my wife, who contributed greatly to this work by tediously reading through the book to edit spelling, grammar, and duplications and to identify any areas that didn't really make sense.

I would also like to thank Carol Ann Rinker, Tom Rhodes, and June Kiss for all the time they spent reviewing this book and calling my attention to sections that needed more information or clarification or had unnecessary duplication, for providing useful suggestions for improvement, and, yes, for pointing out any spelling and grammatical errors they came upon. They were a great help to me and offered some really excellent ideas. I have incorporated most of their corrections and suggestions, and because of their efforts, this is a much-improved work.

Along the way, the encouragement of Adele, Carol Ann, Tom, and June were what I needed to finish this work. I am quite thankful and very appreciative of their efforts.

I would also like to thank Cru and Bill Bright for the development of *Have You Heard of the Four Spiritual Laws?* booklet. This amazing document provided me with a well-developed, concise presentation of the Good News of Jesus Christ.

All scripture passages quoted in this book are taken from the Revised Standard Version of the Bible,[1] unless otherwise noted.

---

[1]. Division of Christian Education of the National Council of the Churches of Christ in the USA, Revised Standard Version New Testament (New York: American Bible Society, 1980), Revised Standard Version Old Testament (New York: American Bible Society, 1973).

INTRODUCTION

For God so loved the world that he gave his only
Son, that whoever believes in him should not
perish but have eternal life.

—John 3:16

One day in April of 1974, I had a life-changing encounter
with Jesus Christ. On that day, he became the Lord
and Savior of my life. It was such an amazing event that I
want to share it with others. Not only do I want to tell them
what happened, but I want those who do not know Jesus to
experience what I experienced.

The purpose of this book then is to tell the story of my
personal encounter with Jesus, the subsequent desire within
me to share him with others, and how that desire came to be
a reality. I also hope that it will encourage others to go out and
share the Good News of Jesus Christ with those who need to
hear it and will help them in some way to do that.

In the Gospel of Mark 10:46–52, Jesus heals Blind
Bartimaeus:

And they came to Jericho; and as he was leaving Jericho with his disciples and a great multitude, Bartimaeus, a blind beggar, the son of Timaeus, was sitting by the roadside. And when he heard that it was Jesus of Nazareth, he began to cry out and say, "Jesus, Son of David, have mercy on me!" And many rebuked him, telling him to be silent; but he cried out all the more, "Son of David, have mercy on me!" And Jesus stopped and said, "Call him." And they called the blind man, saying to him, "Take heart; rise, he is calling you." And throwing off his mantle he sprang up and came to Jesus. And Jesus said to him, "What do you want me to do for you?" And the blind man said to him, "Master, let me receive my sight." And Jesus said to him, "Go your way; your faith has made you well." And immediately he received his sight and followed him on the way.

Before I encountered Jesus, I was very much like blind Bartimaeus—not physically blind but spiritually blind. I had attended church growing up and heard all about Jesus. The problem was that I knew all about Jesus, but I didn't know him personally. When it came to Jesus, I was blind, deaf, and dumb. Then one day, I met Jesus, and he healed me just like he did blind Bartimaeus. Jesus came into my heart as my Lord and Savior. I was born again and became a child of God.

Needless to say, this changed my life. It was wonderful. Naturally, I wanted to share what had happened to me with others. I knew that there were many people out in the world who were spiritually blind, deaf, and dumb just like I had been, even people who attended church like I did. I had no idea of how to share Jesus, but I was sure I was going to do it.

This is my story. I tell how my deep desire to share Jesus became a reality. I share what I went through to reach my goal and how God helped me along the way, making it possible to eventually fulfill this desire. Like most things that occur in life, as I was going through my experiences, I didn't see God's hand in the process, but afterward, looking back, I can see God helping me, guiding me, encouraging me, and making me successful in sharing Jesus in every step along the way.

Throughout my journey, I met many different people. I will tell you about some of them in a later chapter. I also learned many lessons along the way, and I share these with you as well throughout the book. It is my hope that my lessons learned will be beneficial to those who want to share Jesus with those who are lost. The "Lessons Learned" can also be found in Appendix A, where I list them all.

In Part 2, you will find my journal. For the first two years, I went out each day and approached people with the intention of sharing Jesus Christ with them. The journal entries document their reaction when I offered them a Gospel of John.

It is my sincerest hope that anyone with a desire to share Jesus with others will in some way benefit from reading my story, my journal, and my Lessons Learned and that these will help along the way.

In Luke 10:2, Jesus said, "The harvest is plentiful, but the laborers are few; pray therefore the Lord of the harvest to send out laborers into his harvest." I encourage you to help meet the shortage by becoming a laborer in the harvesting of lost souls.

PART 1

How My Ministry Came About

The steps of a man are from the Lord, and he
establishes him in whose way he delights;
though he fall, he shall not be cast headlong, for
the Lord is the stay of his hand.

—Psalm 37:23

Bus Stop Ministry, as I came to call my ministry, came about as a result of my desire to share Jesus with those who don't know him in hope that they will find salvation and everlasting life. I started out from scratch with no idea of how to go about this. I read whatever I could find on the subject, which wasn't much, and I developed an approach. Once I felt ready, I went out and shared Jesus with others.

I wasn't alone in my venture. The Holy Spirit was with me every step of the way. He guided me along the right path and kept me headed in the right direction. My journey is what this book is all about, and I hope it will help and encourage all who want to go out and share the Good News of Jesus Christ.

CHAPTER 1

My Encounter with Christ

> I waited patiently for the Lord; he inclined to me and heard my cry. He drew me up from the desolate pit, out of the miry bog, and set my feet upon a rock, making my steps secure. He put a new song in my mouth, a song of praise to our God.
>
> —Psalm 40:1–3

I was brought up in a Christian home, and as far back as I can remember, I was always taught the Christian way of life. My mother was a very godly person. My father died of polio when I was a year and a half old at which time my mother was pregnant with my younger brother. My mother undertook the task of bringing up three boys. We lived in a double house on the east side of Cleveland, Ohio. My grandmother (Granny) and grandfather (Grandpa) lived upstairs on the second floor, and we lived downstairs on the first floor. It was like a duplex but top and bottom and not side by side like most duplexes today.

Granny was born in Scotland, and Grandpa was from England. I especially remember my Granny. She was a very devout Christian, and she and Grandpa attended a local Baptist church. Granny watched us during the day while my mother was at work. She told us many Bible stories and never missed an opportunity to quote scripture. One of her favorite scriptures was John 3:16, which says, "For God so loved the world that he gave his only Son, that whoever believes in him should not perish but have eternal life." She was always telling us to be good and how much God loved us. Granny liked to listen to the radio and had a religious program tuned in at almost all times. It was usually a preacher preaching a sermon. Her favorite was Cadle Tabernacle. Granny listened to her programs each day while she sat at her kitchen table with a cup of tea.

My mother, when she wasn't at work, spent her time taking care of the house and, even more important, taking care of her three boys. Mom never seemed overly religious, like my Granny did, but you could tell that she had a strong faith and belief in God. I can't imagine what she went through when my father died. She was all alone, unemployed, and pregnant and had to care for me and my older brother. I am sure her faith was tested frequently as she struggled to build a new life—one without my father.

We attended a church down the street. I think it was called the Church of the Redeemer. I don't remember what denomination it was, but Mom faithfully got us up out of bed, dressed, fed, and off to church each Sunday morning. I liked Sunday school. The teachers were great, and we did lots of artsy things, which helped us to learn about Jesus.

When I was a child, I believed in God and his Son, Jesus. However, I didn't understand the Good News and how it applied to me personally. I just went along accepting everything I was told as truth. After all, why would grown-ups tell me something that wasn't true? But when I became a teenager, I began to question things. My mind was full of doubts. I no longer accepted what I was told blindly. I had to reason everything out in my own mind before I could accept it. I tried to reason out God's love, but since I had not experienced it in a personal way, it did not seem logical. As a matter of fact, it seemed to be diametrically opposed to what I saw going on in the world. How could God be loving and at the same time allow all the local gangs to terrorize the neighborhood kids, the bullies, the shoplifters and drug dealers, sickness, suffering, and corruption to exist?

When I was thirteen, Mom purchased a house on the west side of town. As teenagers, three rowdy boys were much more difficult to handle, and I don't think my aging grandparents were up to it. We had become too much for them. I think Grandpa helped Mom with the finances so she could get the house. I know my mother could ill afford this move, but it was necessary.

I didn't see much of my grandparents after that. Once in a while, I would take the Rapid Transit from the west side to the east side of Cleveland to visit friends, and I would sometimes stop in to see Granny. She was always glad to see me. After a short visit, I would leave, but she would always give me a dollar and a Gospel of John and remind me to be a good boy and that God loved me very much. She would also constantly remind me not to get a tattoo because the Bible said that was prohibited. This always set me back because I already had one but was able to hide it from her. I could always use the dollar but the Gospel of John, not so much. I kept it but didn't read it. It usually ended up in my dresser drawer. I had quite a collection of them.

My teenage years were very difficult for me. I rebelled against just about everything, especially if it had to do with religion. I stopped going to church, and I closed my ears when anyone tried to tell me about God. God seemed like such an abstract concept—so far away and unconcerned about me. Anyway, he did not seem to fit into my world, so I proceeded throughout life without him.

Throughout my teenage years and my twenties, my life seemed purposeless. I had no sense of why I was here and where I was going. There was an emptiness within me that just could not be filled. I tried to fill it by pouring myself into my work, but I only found drudgery and boredom. I tried to fill it through sexual pleasures but only found empty relationships. I tried to fill it with alcohol but usually only woke up with a headache the morning after. One morning, I woke up in jail, and I had no idea of what I had done or how I had gotten there. I found out later that I had been in an accident in my automobile. I had had too much to drink but had insisted I was okay to drive. Unfortunately, my friends let me. I had been so drunk that I blacked out. I was conscious but had no idea of what I was doing or where I was going. Finally, I ran into a parked car. That stopped me, but I tried to leave the scene, and I hit the car six times trying to get away. I later found out that the owners of the car I had hit were my mother's friends. I can't imagine how embarrassed she must have been.

I also tried to fill my emptiness with fast and fancy cars but only wound up with speeding tickets and almost lost my license. Every attempt I made to fill the emptiness within me resulted in frustration. Life seemed to be one big disappointment and full of empty promises.

During this period of my life, I experimented with many things, but I always felt that I was in control. I could start or stop anything I did at will. I was in charge. There was one area of my life, however, that seemed to defy this rule. It was an area of my life of which I was not very proud. It involved a bad habit, a sin, which I kept doing, and then afterward, I would experience a great remorse, which became almost too heavy to bear. Each time I committed this sin, I would resolve to break the habit and never do it again. My new resolution would last for a month or two, or maybe even four to six months, but I would ultimately commit the sin again. As time passed, I became more and more concerned over my lack of self-control in this area.

One night, I was sitting in a hotel room in Rochester, New York. I had once again broken my resolution by committing this sin, and I was torn up inside with an unbearable burden of guilt. Deep down within my heart, I was truly sorry for the sin I had committed once again. That evening, in April of 1974, I came to the realization that I was no longer in control, but I was hopelessly enslaved by this sin. No matter what I did to try to stop, I could not.

At that moment, I prayed to God and asked him to help me. I told him I did not want to commit this sin anymore, and I asked him to take control of my life and to deliver me from this sin. It was a simple prayer. I do not even remember the exact words I used, but I do remember the beautiful feeling of peace that came over me. I actually felt the presence of God in the room with me. It was a very powerful feeling, and to this day, I can still remember it. I had never before experienced anything like it. The heavy burden of guilt was instantly lifted from me and taken away. There was a Bible in the room, and I remember reading it and soon after falling into a deep, restful sleep.

That evening, in my hotel room, I experienced for the first time in my life God's love for me, in a very real and personal way. I discovered that God cares for me and wants to have a close, intimate relationship with me.

Since that night, my life has never been the same. I have experienced God's forgiving power in my life. It has been over forty years, and I have never fallen into that sin again. God has delivered me from the crippling power that sin had over me. My heart burns each day with desire to know God better, and I am so thankful that our relationship has been developing over the years and has become stronger. Since that evening, I have had a deep hunger for God's Word, and I spend time with him each day in prayer and scripture study. My greatest desire in life is to please him by doing his will.

I am very happy that you have chosen to read this book. I do not know where you are spiritually, but if you are searching for God and desire to experience his love in a personal way, I want to offer you the opportunity to ask Jesus into your life as Lord and Savior. You do this through prayer. Prayer is simply talking to God. Would you like to pray the following prayer with me now and ask him into your life?

Dear Heavenly Father, help me. I am a sinner, and I am sorry for my sins. I ask you to forgive my sins. I turn away from them and turn to you and ask you to make me the person you want me to be. That is the person I desire to be. I know that Jesus paid the price for all of my sins by dying on the cross for me. Dear Jesus, thank you for dying for me. I open the door of my heart, and I invite you to come in and take control and be the Lord and Savior of my life. From this moment on, I acknowledge you as the Lord and Savior of my life. In Jesus's name. Amen.

If you prayed that prayer, you have been saved.[2] Congratulations! You are born again and now belong to Jesus and are a child of God.

Along with salvation, I received a deep-rooted desire to share this precious gift of Jesus with others. I hope that you share this desire as well and that my book will help you to be successful. In the following chapters, I will tell of the events that led me from having the desire to witness to actually witnessing to others and having the privilege of leading some of them to a personal relationship with Jesus, our Lord and Savior.

I pray that God will richly bless you and give you the courage to go out and share the Good News with all the world.

---

[2]. When people are "saved," it means they have
- admitted they are sinners
- asked God to forgive their sins and deliver them from the consequences of sin
- turned away from their sin (repentance)
- asked Jesus to be the Lord and Savior of their life

As a result of this, they
- have received God's free gift of Grace (which is undeserved)
- have been born again
- are now a child of God
- have a personal relationship with the Lord Jesus Christ
- will spend eternity in the company of the Heavenly Father, Jesus, and all the saints in glory

CHAPTER 2

A Desire to Witness

Go therefore and make disciples of all nations, baptizing them in the name of the Father and of the Son and of the Holy Spirit, teaching them to observe all that I have commanded you; and lo, I am with you always, to the close of the age.

—Matthew 28:19–20

The night I received Jesus as my Lord and Savior, in addition to experiencing the peace that passes understanding, I came away with two deep, burning desires. The first was to read the Bible, which I do each and every day, and the second was a desire to share Jesus and what he had done in my life with others so they could experience the same joy that I did.

My desire to read the Bible was easy to attain. All I had to do was to set a time each day, open the Bible, and read. It has been over forty years since I started doing that, and I still spend time in God's Word every day. I have a reading schedule that I follow each day. It takes me through the entire Bible in a year. It takes about twenty minutes a day.

My second desire was to share my newfound faith. I felt so joyful over the blessing I had received that I wanted to share it with others so they could experience the same joy that I did. Jesus gave marching orders to his twelve apostles when he said, "Preach as you go, saying, 'The kingdom of heaven is at hand. Heal the sick, raise the dead, cleanse lepers, cast out demons. You received without paying, give without pay'" (Matthew 10:7–8). I felt the same way. Freely I had received the goodness of God, and freely I wanted to give back—to share it with others.

While I desired to share my faith, I didn't know how to go about it.

I had observed and read stories about some of the great evangelists like Billy Graham, Billy Sunday, and Dwight Moody and was quite encouraged, even energized, at the thought of their bringing hundreds to the Lord at each of their crusades. I knew I wasn't equipped for that. I had watched other evangelists on television and at Christian gatherings as they offered to pray with people for salvation. This also was beyond my scope. I was thinking more of a one-on-one approach to evangelism. At the time, I had no clue that it wasn't these evangelists who brought the people to the point where they were presented the Good News but God who was leading his children who had gone astray to the point where they were able to make a decision for Christ. God simply used these evangelists to achieve his purpose.

My desire to share Jesus was a bit more complicated than preaching to a large group of people, even though I was pretty sure I would never be able to do that. It was more difficult because it meant I would have to approach people, begin a conversation, incorporate the Good News in the conversation, and then ask them if they wanted to pray with me and accept Jesus Christ as their Lord and Savior.

This was difficult because I am basically a shy person, an introvert by nature, and don't generally like to try to "sell" something to another person. I also had no idea of how I would go about this or if I would be successful. As a young boy, I delivered newspapers, and whenever the paper had a "new subscription" drive, they would encourage their newspaper delivery boys to knock on doors to sell subscriptions. There were prizes for selling subscriptions. The more you sold, the better the prize. I knocked on a lot of doors and made my approach but don't remember signing anyone up, nor do I remember being awarded any prizes.

As I thought more about my reluctance to share Jesus, it basically came down to fear. My fears included

- not knowing scripture well enough
- not being a good enough salesman
- being afraid that people would think I was a Jehovah's Witness or some kind of a fanatic
- knowing that I would be rejected by some and wondering how I would deal with that rejection

What if someone saw me witnessing? A friend, a neighbor, an acquaintance, a coworker? What would I do or say?

I did a great deal of soul searching and talking to God. Even though I wasn't sure of myself, I decided I wanted to, needed to, and was going to overcome my fears and do this. I knew that I had my Heavenly Father's approval and that I would receive his guidance and help along the way. Nothing else mattered.

I searched the Christian bookstores for some kind of a guide to sharing Jesus but didn't find anything to help me. I remember talking to a clerk at a Christian bookstore about it, and she wasn't able to provide any guidance. She did mention that one way of witnessing was by example, by the way we live our lives. The idea, which is a good one, is that if you live a good Christian life, others will see that, want to know what it is all about, and then possibly ask you to explain it. This would give you an opportunity to tell them about Jesus. Her suggestion brought to mind St. Francis's quote: "Preach Jesus, and if necessary, use words." I liked the concept, but honestly, I was looking for something much more radical that would yield greater results. It didn't have to be like a Billy Graham crusade, where hundreds came forward at the altar call. My goal was much simpler. If I was able to lead one person to Jesus, I would have met my goal and been successful. Of course, I wouldn't stop there, but that was my initial goal.

Once in a while, as I traveled through Washington DC, going to and from work, I would encounter a street evangelist preaching to the crowd. I didn't think I was mature enough or knowledgeable enough or had courage enough to preach to crowds on the street. I wanted to witness on a one-to-one basis and felt quite sure that I could do that. I just needed to figure out how to go about it. I prayed about this, asking for God's help. I knew that I was called to do this, just as all Christians are. Jesus said to his disciples, "The harvest is plentiful, but the laborers are few; pray therefore the Lord of the harvest to send out laborers into his harvest" (Matthew 9:37–38). I deeply desired to be a laborer in the harvest. I just needed help working out the mechanics of how to do it.

I had joined a church after my conversion. It was Christian but not evangelical. They preached the social gospel and were very concerned with social justice. I really enjoyed the people, and the Bible study was great, but I didn't find any help with my desire to witness.

After searching for considerable time, I did finally find a book on evangelism, which was helpful, but it was more slanted toward starting an evangelism program in your church. I wasn't ready for that, and I was pretty sure my church wasn't either. One concept that I remember from reading the book was that you need to be able to present the gospel message quickly and concisely. If I remember correctly, you should be able to do this in two or three minutes. This was because it might be all of the time you would have to share Jesus with a nonbeliever.

As I look back, I can see that all that I went through was part of the process God was working in me to get me to the place I wanted so much to be. Of course, it was where God wanted me to be as well, but he did it with such gentleness and patience.

My wife and I had joined a prayer group, which I thoroughly enjoyed. I especially liked the praise music and the Bible sharing that they had each week. We became a part of the prayer group's ministry to the elderly. It was called Village House. A ministry team made up of a few of the prayer group members would visit an assisted living home each Sunday and socialize with the residents. Then we would sing some of the old-time gospel hymns that the residents knew so well and loved, and one of the prayer group members would give a Bible-based sharing. The meeting would wind up with time to pray for their needs.

After a while, I was asked if I would like to prepare and share a message. I jumped at the offer and prepared a message on the Twenty-Third Psalm. The message was well received by all, and I was invited to present it at the prayer meeting. It went well, and I became a regular presenter. I would prepare and present a message every two or three months. This didn't make me a better evangelist, but it did help me in my study of God's Word. It also made me more courageous in sharing Jesus. I experienced a great deal of personal growth during this time.

In December of 1990, I did a sharing entitled "You Are the Hands and Feet of Jesus." One of the main scriptures I used in this sharing was Romans 10:9–15, which says,

> If you confess with your lips that Jesus is Lord and believe in your heart that God raised him from the dead, you will be saved. For man believes with his heart and so is justified, and he confesses with his lips and so is saved. The scripture says, "No one who believes in him will be put to shame." For there is no distinction between Jew and Greek; the same Lord is Lord of all and bestows his riches upon all who call upon him. For, "every one who calls upon the name of the Lord will be saved." But how are men to call

> upon him in whom they have not believed? And how are they to believe in him of whom they have never heard? And how are they to hear without a preacher? And how can men preach unless they are sent? As it is written, "How beautiful are the feet of those who preach good news!"

From this scripture, I concluded that if a messenger goes out, the message will be proclaimed. If the message is proclaimed, then the people will hear. If the people hear, they will believe. If the people believe, then they will call upon the Lord. If they call upon the Lord, then they will be born again and become a child of God. It all starts with getting the message out. All believers are called to do this. We are the hands and feet of Jesus.

While in the process of preparing and presenting this message, I renewed my desire to share Jesus with others and deepened my desire to witness.

One of my hobbies is leather work, and for Christmas (1990), I prepared a leather key ring with the company logo on it to give each of my staff. I wanted to give them a personal gift and had the great idea to include something about Jesus with it. After all, this was the perfect time since Christmas celebrates the birth of Jesus. I searched for a biblical tract that would tell about Jesus and found *Bread of Life*,[3] which is a stand-alone Gospel of John (the one on the cover of this book). After becoming a Christian, I came to see the wisdom of my grandmother who gave me all those Gospels of John.

My leather key ring was well received, but nobody said anything about the Gospel of John. I was okay with that. I liked the *Bread of Life* booklet. Since I was handing out the Gospel of John, just giving it away, I began to call it a "Gift." It seemed to me to be a great tool for sharing the Good News.

I was so convinced that this was a great tool for witnessing that I ordered a hundred copies from the publisher. My idea was to give a copy to all I would meet. They took about a week

---

[3] *Bread of Life* Copyright © 1985 by Thomas Nelson, Inc.

to arrive in the mail. Meanwhile, I thought and prayed about how and where I would hand them out. When they arrived, my plan was to prayerfully distribute the Gifts. I would ask God to guide me and to use them for his purpose. I wanted him to show me where I could distribute them and exactly how I would go about doing it. They finally came, and I was ready.

The Saturday after the Gifts arrived, I took some of them with me when I went out to run a few errands. I went to the supermarket with a handful of Gifts. I wasn't sure where to give them out or how to approach people. If I remember correctly, I just held the Gift out, offering it to passersby. I didn't get many takers. I began to wonder if this was legal to do in front of a supermarket. After all, it was soliciting. I didn't want to get in trouble with the supermarket staff, especially the manager, and I certainly didn't want to get in trouble with the police. I didn't stay very long, nor did I give out very many Gifts. I came away quite discouraged.

I went to the barbershop for a haircut. When my barber finished cutting my hair, I gave him a Gift. He took it and thanked me. He seemed genuinely interested. As I was leaving, I heard my barber telling one of the other barbers about the Gift as he showed it to him. This greatly increased my excitement about the value of witnessing, and I came to realize the multiplication effect.

Lesson Learned #7[4]

The Multiplication Effect — Some who received the Gift would share it with friends and family because they just thought it was a nice gift or because they thought the person they shared it with needed to hear the message.

---

[4]. Throughout my ministry, I learned quite a few lessons about sharing Jesus with others. I am including them because I think they will be helpful for those of you who will go out and share the Good News. I call these "Lessons Learned." They are interspersed throughout the book, and I have included a complete list in Appendix A.

After leaving the barbershop, I decided to go over to one of the larger stores in the shopping center with the intention of giving away all the Gifts I had brought with me.

I handed out eleven Gifts to all those who passed by. It only took a few minutes. My approach was to ask each person if he or she would like a free Gift as I handed it out. Most of those I asked smiled and took the Gift. I was ready and willing to share Jesus with anyone who asked. No one did. One fellow asked, "What is that for?" when I handed it to him. I told him it was a Gospel of John, and he said, "No!"

After handing out all the Gifts I had, I went home feeling really excited. I prayed that each person who received a Gift would read it and come to know Jesus as his or her Lord and Savior.

The next Saturday, I went to the Wonder Bread store, and as I was checking out, I offered a Gift to the clerk. She took it and thanked me. Then she said, "You know I am Catholic." I wasn't quite sure why this mattered. I responded, "So am I. Where do you go to Mass?" She didn't give me the name of her church but said it was in Laurel, Maryland.

Lesson Learned #8

At the Wonder Bread store, I was given the opportunity to share my faith with someone who just happened to be of the same faith community as me. Throughout this ministry, I had the opportunity to share with people of many other faith backgrounds—Baptists, Evangelicals, Mormons, Jehovah's Witnesses, those of the Jewish and Islamic faiths, and others. I took an interest in learning what others believed, and then, when given the opportunity, I used that knowledge to share the Good News with them. It became easier as time went on, and as my knowledge increased, I became better prepared and more proficient at sharing the Good News.

After leaving the Wonder Bread store, I went to the bank and gave a Gift to the bank teller. She said, "Thanks," and smiled.

A few days later, I had to take my daughter to a shopping center to meet her friend. They were going to do something together, and I decided I would wait for her and hand out Gifts. I did so for a while, but the same concerns popped up regarding solicitations, store managers, and police. I also wasn't quite sure how I would explain what I was doing to my daughter should she return and see me handing out the Gospel of John.

And so, the dilemma. Deep down, I wanted to witness and share my faith. I had found a great tool to do that, the Gospel of John, but at the same time, I didn't want to get into any trouble for soliciting where I didn't think it was permitted. I don't remember when or how, but it finally came to me. I somehow made a great discovery (thank you, Lord). It occurred to me that I could hand out my Gifts at any one of the many metro stations, and since I rode the metro just about every day, it would be very convenient. This thought gave birth to Bus Stop Ministry. It seemed to be the way to go but how? I wasn't quite sure. I needed to come up with a better, more thought-out plan.

CHAPTER 3

My Plan for Sharing the Good News

A man's mind plans his way, but the Lord directs his steps.

—Proverbs 16:9

Just to reiterate, I had a deep desire to share Jesus with others. I wanted them to experience what I had in my hotel room in Rochester, New York, when I accepted Jesus Christ as my Lord and Savior. That was my motivation, but I needed God's help. I knew what I wanted to do but didn't quite know how to do it. It would have been nice to hear directly from God, but I knew that God didn't usually work that way. Proverbs 16:1–3 says, "The plans of the mind belong to man, but the answer of the tongue is from the Lord. All the ways of a man are pure in his own eyes, but the Lord weighs the spirit. Commit your work to the Lord, and your plans will be established."   The plan in my mind was to share the

Good News with anyone interested. I knew that my motives were pure. I wanted others to know and accept Jesus as their Lord and Savior so they could know the goodness of God. So I committed this to the Lord. I knew that somehow not only would my plan be established but that God would make it successful.

Initially, I planned to hand out a Gospel of John (Gift) to everyone I came in contact with, but after a few failed attempts at the supermarket and the mall, I realized that I needed a better plan. That was when my new plan of passing my Gifts out at a metro station surfaced. I guess this was just the Lord directing my steps. I had seen others passing out things at a metro station—from samples of yogurt and drink cups to political advertisements, so why not the Good News of Jesus Christ? There were many stations and thousands of people passed through each station every morning and evening. I could easily distribute my Gifts at any of the stations and could visit different stations, each with its own audience.

I decided to start at the Rosslyn Metro Train Station. The station is a gathering place for people from all walks of life. They arrive each day because it is a waystation where they are forced to pause and await their next connection as they journey on to their daily destination. People of all different ages, races, nationalities, income levels, and statuses in life show up, spend a short time, and then move on.

There were others who worked at the station, either for the metro, at one of the convenience stores, or in some vending capacity—the station master, bus drivers, vendors, and so on.

The station was also a hangout for numerous homeless people. They would show up and panhandle throughout the day. And then there were the regulars who came each day, or as often as they could, to spend time with the other regulars and deepen their friendships.

Tivoli's coffee shop was right there, and many gathered for morning coffee and fresh pastry before heading off to work or wherever their day was to take them.

There were a number of stores, fast-food places, and restaurants surrounding the Rosslyn Station, and many of the people would walk by the station during their lunch break as they went to and from their places of work to buy lunch and shop at the drugstore or other retail stores. They went by pretty quickly. I had lots of opportunities to offer them a Gift.

Occasionally, there would be some maintenance workers at the station or repairing the streets. They also would receive an offer of a free Gift.

All in all, the Rosslyn Metro Train Station was a great place to share Jesus. People from all walks of life would pass by each day, and many were glad to receive a free Gift and to hear about the Good News of Jesus Christ.

Once I started, I spent most of my lunchtime at the Rosslyn Metro Station. It was only a few minutes from work. I decided I would stand near the escalator, and as people approached, I would say, "I'd like to give you a free Gift," while at the same time handing them a Gift. This wasn't too realistic, as I quickly found out, because people entering a metro station are in a hurry to get to the platform where they can catch the next train home. I altered my plan to just extend out my hand with a Gift in it.

It usually didn't take very long at all, and all my Gifts would be gone. This was great! I felt so good getting out the Word of God without breaking any laws. I continued to do this, but after a while, I began to wonder how I could get people involved in a discussion. I wanted to share my personal experience with Jesus, and just handing them a Gift was too fast paced. Once in a while, someone would stop to talk, but it was the exception rather than the rule.

One day, it came to me (or possibly it was the Lord directing my next step). I wanted to find a time when people had nothing to do so I could start a conversation. I realized that the metro station was also a bus terminal. Quite a few busses from different routes stopped at the Rosslyn Station. People got off the incoming bus and either entered the metro or connected with another bus. There were also people who exited the metro and caught a connecting bus. A captive audience—people standing around or sitting on a bench with nothing to do but wait for their bus. What a great opportunity!

After some trial and error, I figured out that the best way to share my Gifts would be to sit on one of the bus stop benches just outside the Rosslyn Metro Train Station entrance and wait for someone to sit down next to me. It didn't take very long. I didn't want to be rude, so when people sat down and were reading a book or the newspaper, I wouldn't bother them. If they sat down and seemingly had nothing to do except wait for their bus, I would approach them by saying, "Hi, I'd like to give you a free Gift." If they said, "No, thanks," I would leave them alone. If they seemed interested, I would give them a Gift and then share the Good News with them. I knew I would most likely be limited time wise because their bus would soon arrive, so I needed a way to present the Good News in a quick, efficient way.

I was familiar with a great tool for sharing the Good News of Jesus Christ called the *Four Spiritual Laws*.[5] I don't remember where I first heard about it, but I was quite impressed with it.

The following gives some background on the *Four Spiritual Laws*, and it is taken from an article I found in *Wikipedia*, the free encyclopedia, titled "Cru (Christian organization)."

Four Spiritual Laws[6]

In 1959, Bill Bright developed the Four Spiritual Laws talking points in consultation with the salesman Bob Ringer after he and his team encountered difficulty disseminating the Gospel message. In 1965, the Toledo businessman Gus Yeager took the initiative to compile the Four Spiritual Laws into a booklet, which was accompanied by supporting Bible verses, some

---

5. From *Have You Heard of the Four Spiritual Laws?* written by Bill Bright, ©1965-2019 The Bright Media Foundation and Campus Crusade for Christ, Inc. All rights reserved. http://crustore.org/four-spiritual-laws-online/ Included by permission.
6. Written by Bill Bright. ©Copyright 1965 Campus Crusade for Christ, Inc. All rights reserved. Simultaneously published in Canada. Manufactured in the United States of America.

commentary, and support diagrams. Bright had large quantities of the booklet printed and distributed in campuses across the United States. These Four Spiritual Laws presented a concise, four-step process of how to become a Christian and became one of the most widely distributed religious booklets in history. By 2006, the booklet had been translated into over 200 languages and more than 2.5 billion copies had been distributed worldwide. Due to its simplicity, it continues to be used in various forms by Cru and its international affiliates.

The *Four Spiritual Laws* consist of the following points:

- God loves you and offers a wonderful plan for your life.
- Man is sinful and separated from God. Thus he cannot know and experience God's love and plan for his life.
- Jesus Christ is God's provision for man's sin. Through him, you can know and experience God's love and plan for your life.
- We must individually receive Jesus Christ as Savior and Lord; then we can know and experience God's love and plan for our lives.

Using the *Four Spiritual Laws* as a tool, I developed the basic approach outlined in the next chapter.

CHAPTER 4

The Approach

Always be prepared to make a defense to any
one who calls you to account for the hope that is
in you, yet do it with gentleness and reverence.

—1 Peter 3:15

When you approach someone to share the Good News, if
you want to be successful, you have to spend some time
beforehand preparing how you are going to do this and what
you are going to say.

Lesson Learned #1

If you want to share the Good News of Jesus Christ, you need to first prepare. This preparation consists of developing the following:

- Approach—how will you approach the person to whom you are going to witness?
- Present—how can you quickly and efficiently share the Good News? (What are you going to say, and how are you going to say it?)
- Ask—after presenting the Gospel, how will you ask them if they would like to make a commitment to receive Jesus Christ as their Lord and Savior?
- Pray for those who say yes—What prayer will you use? Prepare one in advance and memorize it.
- For those who say no, leave the door open. Give them a *Four Spiritual Laws* booklet to take away with them and hope they will read and think about it.
- For those who receive Jesus, share the four things to focus on from chapter 4.
- Close—this will be different for those who accept Jesus and those who don't.

I am not a salesman, but every salesman knows that if he doesn't prepare, he won't make the sale. However, witnessing is a bit different than making a sale. Many principles are the same, but there are some marked distinctions.

The biggest difference is that the Holy Spirit is involved. My part is to have a desire to share Jesus and to be prepared to do so on a moment's notice, in an efficient and effective way. The Holy Spirit will bring to me those who, deep down within themselves, are searching for God but don't know how or where to find him. He will also bring those who are ready to make a commitment to accept and follow Jesus, once they learn how. I realized that that's my job. Apostle Paul in 1 Corinthians 3:6–7 says, "I planted, Apollos watered, but God gave the growth. So neither he who plants nor he who waters is anything, but only God who gives the growth."   God is working in the hearts of all the unsaved. His goal is that all should be saved, but he will never violate their free will in the process. I was ready to play a part, a very important part, of that process by sharing Jesus. The person I approached might not accept Jesus as a result of my presentation, but I knew I could rest assured that I would have touched his or her heart in some way, and he or she would be much closer to making a decision to follow Jesus than he or she was before I witnessed. Some plant, some water, but God gives the growth, and I was ready to do any of the above.

Like in any good presentation, I realized that once I had prepared what I would say and do, I would need to practice my presentation. This I knew would yield a smooth presentation and build up my confidence.

Lesson Learned #2

Practice, practice, practice your presentation.

During my years of Bus Stop Ministries, I used something like the following approach. I was always trying to improve it, so it changed often. Also, for each person I witnessed to, the approach was altered to fit the situation. I depended upon the Holy Spirit for guidance. What you see here is kind of a template that I modified to fit the specific situation and the person I had encountered. It was somewhat extemporaneous, and my approach varied with every situation. My reason for presenting it here is to give you a good idea of how it went.

When I approached people with the intention of sharing the Good News, I would say, "Hi, I'd like to give you a free Gift." If they came back with a negative response, I would just back off and leave them alone. If they were receptive, they would usually respond with something like, "Sure, what is it?" I would respond with, "It is a Gospel of John; it's from the Bible." Next, I would say, "The Gospel of John was written by the apostle John, who was one of Jesus's closest followers, and in it, he tells all about the Good News of Jesus Christ."

Then, I would ask, "Are you familiar with the Good News of Jesus Christ?" If they said they weren't familiar with the Good News, I would ask if they had a minute so I could explain it to them. If they said that they didn't have time, I would give them the Gift, encourage them to read it, and then move on. If they did have time, I would continue on with my presentation.

If they said they were already familiar with the Good News of Jesus Christ, I would preface my explanation with, "Great! I would like to get your thoughts on my presentation of the Good News." The goal here is to get them to listen to the presentation of the Good News of Jesus Christ, whether or not they said they knew what the Good News was. For those who were already Christians and familiar with the Good News, I was hoping for some positive, helpful input regarding my presentation.

To accomplish this, I would go through the *Four Spiritual Laws* talking points with them. I would start by saying, "I am going to use the *Four Spiritual Laws* talking points, developed by Dr. Bill Bright. The four laws make it easier to understand the Good News. Each of the talking points is supported with verses from scripture, from the Bible."

If they said they didn't want to, I would simply give them a copy of the *Four Spiritual Laws* to complement their Gospel of John and encourage them to read it on their own, and they would go on their way. If they said yes, then I would begin.

I made it a point to memorize the *Four Spiritual Laws* as well as the accompanying scripture referred to in the booklet. That way, as we worked our way through the *Four Spiritual Laws*, I could recite them instead of reading them, and I would have an opportunity to look at the people and see how they were receiving what I was saying. Then, if necessary, I could make modifications to my presentation.

I began with the first law by saying, "The first law says, 'God loves you and offers a wonderful plan for your life.' The first scripture is from the Gospel of John chapter 3 verse 16, where Jesus says, 'For God so loved the world that he gave his only Son, that whoever believes in him should not perish but have eternal life.'" Then I would explain that God loves the world, which includes both of us, so much that he was willing to sacrifice his only son to pay the penalty for our sins so that we could have eternal life. Next, I would say, "The second scripture for law 1 is from the Gospel of John, chapter 10, verse 10, where Jesus said, 'The thief comes only to steal and kill and destroy; I came that they may have life, and have it abundantly.'"

Then I would point out, "As you read the first spiritual law and the scriptures that go with it, which talk about God's love and wonderful plan for us, and try to relate it to the world as it is today, you can't help but notice that there is a real disconnect. Sure God loves us and has a wonderful plan for our lives, but what about all the corruption in the world today—the gangs, terrorists, teenage shooters, bullies, drug dealers, pornography, prostitution, cybercrime, elder abuse, human trafficking, and so on? How do you resolve this?"

Next, I would say, "The second law helps us to understand the disconnect. It says, 'Man is sinful and separated from God. Thus, he cannot know and experience God's love and plan for his life.'"

As we discussed the second law, I would quote the first scripture reference. I would say, "In the book of Romans, chapter 3, verse 23, the Bible says, '*All* [emphasize not some but all] have sinned and fall short of the glory of God.' So the disconnect is caused by man's sinfulness, and as a result of that sin, he is separated and far away from God. In the booklet, there is a diagram showing sinful man on one side and Holy God on the other, and there is a great gap between them." I would use this to explain that sinful man tries to bridge the gap by being a nice person, doing nice things for others, being religious, going to church, but he always falls short. Then I would share the second verse for law 2 from Romans, chapter 6, verse 23, which says, "'For the wages of sin is *death, but* [emphasis on these two words] the free gift of God is eternal life in Christ Jesus our Lord.' So there is a way back for sinful man to Holy God, and that way is through

Jesus Christ. As a matter of fact, the third law says, 'Jesus Christ is God's only provision for man's sin. Through him, you can know and experience God's love and plan for your life.'"

Next, I would say, "The first scripture for law 3 is from Romans, chapter 5, verse 8, which says, 'God shows his love for us in that while we were yet sinners Christ died for us.' That's how much God loves us. Even though we have sinned and are separated from him because of it, he still loves us and sent his only son, Jesus, to die on the cross to pay the penalty for our sins so we can be reunited with him."

Then I would say, "The second scripture for law 3 is from the Gospel of John, chapter 14, verse 6, in which Jesus says, 'I am the way, and the truth, and the life; no one comes to the Father, but by me.' Jesus is telling us that he is the way back to the Father."

Next, I would tell them, "But it is not enough to know these things, or even to mentally assent to them. Law 4 tells us, 'We must individually receive Jesus Christ as Savior and Lord. Then we can know and experience God's love and plan for our lives.'"

"The Bible tells us in the Gospel of John, chapter 1, verses 12–13, that 'All who received him, who believed in his name, he gave power to become children of God; who were born, not of blood nor of the will of the flesh nor the will of man, but of God.'" Then I would say, "So by accepting Jesus by faith as Lord and Savior, you are born again, and become a child of God." To further clarify this, I would quote Ephesians, chapter 2, verses 8–9, which says, "For by grace you have been saved through faith; and this is not your own doing, it is the gift of God—not because of works, lest any man should boast." Then I would continue, "When, by faith, you accept Jesus as Lord and Savior, God gives you the free gift of his grace and you are born again and become a child of God."

Then I would tell them, "In Revelation, chapter 3, verse 20, Jesus says, 'Behold, I stand at the door and knock; if any one hears my voice and opens the door, I will come in to him and eat with him, and he with me.' There is a famous painting that was done depicting this scripture by William Holman Hunt.

He calls it *The Light of the World*. In his painting, he shows Jesus in a garden scene, knocking on a cottage door. The really interesting thing about the painting is that the door has no handle. What Mr. Hunt is portraying is that Jesus will not yank open the door to your heart and barge his way into your life. He can't; there is no door handle. No, you must open the door of your heart from the inside and invite him in."

Then I would tell them, "You can do this by prayer. Prayer is simply talking to God." Next, I would ask them the key question, "Would you like to pray and invite Jesus into your heart as Lord and Savior?" If they said no, I would give them the *Four Spiritual Laws* booklet, ask them to review it, and tell them if they changed their minds, it would tell them what to do.

If they said yes, I would ask them to repeat after me, praying the following prayer:

> Dear Heavenly Father, I am sorry for my sins. (Repeat.) I ask you to forgive me for my sins. (Repeat.) Make me the person you want me to be. (Repeat.) That's the person I want to be. (Repeat.) Dear Lord Jesus, I open the door of my heart, and I invite you in to be my Lord and Savior. (Repeat.)

Then I would tell them, "Now that you have prayed that prayer, you have been saved. In Romans, chapter 10, verse 9, the Bible says, 'If you confess with your lips that Jesus is Lord [which you did], and believe in your heart that God raised him from the dead [which you do], you will be saved [which you were]. For man believes with his heart and so is justified, and he confesses with his lips and so is saved.'"

Then I would say, "Now that you have been saved, there are four things that I would like you to focus on," and I would share the following items:

1. The first thing is to spend some time each day reading the Bible. The Bible is God's love letter to you, but you

have to read it to discover what God has to say to you. I suggest you start with the Gospel of John that I gave you. It's a very good place to start. Each day, set aside a time and find a quiet place. Read a page or paragraph or so, whatever you have time for. How much you read is not as important as establishing the daily reading habit. After reading, take a few moments to reflect on what you have read. How has God spoken to you through your reading? Also, now that you are a child of God, you should read the Bible as a participant and no longer as an observer. In other words, now that you are a Christian, you are no longer just observing what Christians do. Now you will read and respond as Christians do.

2. The second thing is to take time to pray each day. Prayer is simply talking to God. Spend time in conversation with God. You can talk to God about anything, anytime, anywhere. You should set aside a time each day, find a quiet place, and start a conversation with God. Tell him what's going on in your life: the good things, the bad things, the happy things, the sad things. Tell him your concerns, ask him your questions, and intercede for those you are worried about, those who need help and healing. Since a conversation is two-sided, talking and listening, after you have said what you have to say, stop, be still, and listen to what he has to say in response to your prayer. Also, remember that the Lord gave you two ears and one mouth. Use them in that ratio.

3. The third thing is to find a local church where there are other brothers and sisters who believe in Jesus as you do. They will support and encourage you as you will them. Take your time in doing this. You don't have to run out and join a church. Visit different churches. Talk to the parishioners and the pastor. Attend a service and whatever else they offer: Sunday school, a prayer meeting, a Bible Study. When you find a church

you are comfortable with, join it and become an active member.

4. The fourth thing I would like you to do is to tell others about Jesus. You don't have to be a Biblical scholar or have a theological degree to tell others about Jesus. In the second book of Corinthians, chapter 5, verse 17, the Bible says, "Therefore, if any one is in Christ, he is a new creation; the old has passed away, behold, the new has come." You are a new person in Christ Jesus. Some things you did before, you will no longer be interested in doing. Other things you have never done, like reading the Bible and praying each day, you will begin to do. Others will notice the change. When they ask you about it, use the opportunity to share with them what Jesus has done for you and what he means to you.

This was my basic approach. Each person I encountered was different, and I had to modify the approach to suit the situation. Since I had the basic approach down, it wasn't difficult at all to modify it for each person as needed.

Now that I had worked out my approach, I was ready to go, but there was another issue that I had to overcome, which I will address in the next chapter.

CHAPTER 5

Additional Reservations about Witnessing

How beautiful are the feet of those who preach good news!

—Romans 10:15

With my basic approach worked out, I should have been ready to go out and share Jesus, but there was an additional reservation that I had to deal with—the possibility of rejection.

When I first started handing out Gifts, I was very concerned about people who didn't take the Gift. I couldn't understand why they would refuse my free gift. I soon realized that many who refused the Gift may not have had any idea what it was, and they simply didn't want to be bothered. Lots of advertisement flyers are handed out at the metro, and riders, me included, often are in a hurry to get somewhere, are not interested in what is being offered, and just refuse to take the flyer.

After thinking this through, I was okay with that type of rejection, but I still felt concerned by those who knew what it was and refused the Gift. Then I discovered a passage in Luke 10:16, where Jesus said, "He who hears you hears me, and he who rejects you rejects me, and he who rejects me rejects him who sent me." After meditating on this verse, I realized that anyone who responded in a negative way to my offer of a free Gift and knew what it was was not rejecting me but rejecting God. I needed to learn not to take that rejection personally. This was hard for me because I always found it very sad when someone rejected God's free gift. I should have been more forgiving, considering the number of times I rejected my grandmother's frequent offers. I really wanted people to accept Jesus as their Lord and Savior.

Lesson Learned #3

There will be rejection. Some people will refuse a Gift because they don't know what it is and don't want to be bothered. Others may know what it is and reject it. In this case, realize that they are not rejecting you, but they are rejecting God (see Luke 10:16).

The passage from Luke helped me to understand that I wasn't being rejected, but God was. If you take these rejections personally, it won't be long before you are beaten down and ready to give up. I had to remember that I was God's delivery person. I was just the messenger. God was using me to get the message out to those who needed to hear it. I could never know what the other person was thinking when I approached him or her. I learned quickly that there would be those who simply rejected the offer. More complicated were those who appeared to do so, but deep down within them, something amazing was happening. The message I brought to them was touching their hearts—maybe not immediately, but as they thought about their encounter with me, they were moved. I tried not to focus on outward appearances. Instead, I came to realize that it was what was going on inside of people that was really important.

With all the rejection, it's easy to get discouraged when witnessing. I sometimes feel sorry for the Mormons who go door to door. Usually, there are two young men, and all they want to do is share their faith. I am certain that they get a great deal of rejection. When they come to my door, I always take the time to listen to what they have to say. Most people don't want to be bothered. The truth of the matter is that Satan doesn't want any more Christians than there already are, so he will do whatever he can to discourage you and those you approach.

Even so, it seemed that whenever I felt the least bit discouraged, I would be surprised by God.

Lesson Learned #5

When I was witnessing on a daily basis, there were some days when nothing appeared to happen (dry spell). Even though I didn't see anything happening, I needed to be assured that God was working. My job was to hand out the Gospel of John. God is using me for that purpose. Sometimes during a dry spell, I was all of sudden surprised by God. God caused something to happen when I least expected it, and as a result, I was richly blessed. Being surprised by God is not only amazing, but his surprises were confirmations that I was doing what I was supposed to be doing.

For example, I was on the metro one day (not sure if I was going to or coming from work), and I saw a man reading a Gospel of John. It looked like the one I was handing out at the time. I couldn't help myself, and I asked him where he got the Gospel of John. He told me that his girlfriend had received it from someone who was handing them out and she gave it to him. I was ecstatic. He was reading God's Word, and I knew it would touch his heart. I wondered how many of the thousands of Gifts that I handed out had been passed on to others. This really clarified for me that I just didn't and wouldn't know what happened to the Gifts that I distributed. But then it didn't really matter that I knew. What was important was that God knew and was using Bus Stop Ministry and the Gifts to touch the hearts of others for him.

Our Heavenly Father had set up a divine appointment with each person I approached. I didn't know what the outcome would be, but God did. My job was to present the message. I could be sure God would do the rest.

It turned out that I found that rejection kindled the fire within me to share the Good News of Jesus Christ. Rejection of God's gift was real, but so was acceptance, and that provided the motivation for going out and sharing God's Good News.

I struggled with all of this and didn't want to be hurt by rejection, but my even deeper desire was to witness. This was my heart's desire. I wanted to be a "laborer in the vineyard." I wanted others to have and experience what I had when I accepted Jesus as my Lord and Savior and to know how wonderful it is each day to be in a right relationship with Jesus. I knew that if I didn't go out and witness, that desire would be lost. I didn't know how many would accept Jesus as their Lord and Savior as a result of my witnessing, but I knew I wanted and had to go out.

After working this all out in my mind, I was okay with rejection and ready to move on. I was ready to go out and share the Good News!

CHAPTER 6

The Parable of the Sower

*The condition of the heart determines how the
Good News of Jesus Christ will be received.*

I discovered that sharing the Good News with those you don't
know will produce different and varying results. Some are
ready to receive the message, and others are not. You really
can't tell how someone will receive what you have to offer,
so you have to just go forth and proclaim the Good News
and see how it is received. God works in the hearts of the
unsaved to bring them to the point of accepting the Good
News, but he needs someone to go out and share the message.
All Christians are called to do this—to share the Good News
with the unsaved. Whether it is received is not up to you. It
is up to them, and it all depends on where they are in their
spiritual walk. Jesus tells us about this in the Parable of the
Sower (The Gospel of Luke, chapter 8). Remember that Jesus's
parables serve two purposes. First of all, they are interesting
stories for all who hear them. Second, they contain a deeper
meaning for all those who are seeking the Kingdom of God.

In Luke 8:4–8 Jesus says,

> And when a great crowd came together and people from town after town came to him, he said in a parable: "A sower went out to sow his seed; and as he sowed, some fell along the path, and was trodden under foot, and the birds of the air devoured it. And some fell on the rock; and as it grew up, it withered away, because it had no moisture. And some fell among thorns; and the thorns grew with it and choked it. And some fell into good soil and grew, and yielded a hundredfold." As he said this, he called out, "He who has ears to hear, let him hear."

It was a nice story that I am sure appealed to Jesus's agricultural crowd, but there was also a deeper meaning. The seed is the Word of God. The sower is the one who sows the seed—sharing the Word of God. The ground represents the heart of the one who receives the Word of God from the sower. Note that in each example, God's Word is received differently.

In part 2 (Luke 8:10–15), the apostles ask for the deeper meaning, and Jesus tells them,

> To you it has been given to know the secrets of the kingdom of God; but for others they are in parables, so that seeing they may not see, and hearing they may not understand. Now the parable is this: The seed is the word of God. The ones along the path are those who have heard; then the devil comes and takes away the word from their hearts, that they may not believe and be saved. And the ones on the rock are those who, when they hear the word, receive it with joy; but these have no root, they believe for a while and in time of temptation fall away. And as for what fell among the thorns, they are those who hear, but as they go on their way they are

choked by the cares and riches and pleasures of life, and their fruit does not mature. And as for that in the good soil, they are those who, hearing the word, hold it fast in an honest and good heart, and bring forth fruit with patience.

Jesus's disciples asked Jesus what the parable meant. They were looking for the deeper meaning. Jesus told his disciples that the different ground conditions (conditions of the heart) determined how the seed (the Word of God) was received. The Word was not able to penetrate those with hard hearts (hard ground) because the Devil took it away from them immediately before it could grow and bear fruit. Those with hearts like rocky ground allowed the seed to grow, but it soon died off because the rocky ground prevented the seed from growing deep roots. Their newfound joy disappeared when they gave in to the devil's temptation, and he sucked them back into their old ways. Those with thorny hearts allowed the Word to take root with joy, but the devil choked it out with the cares and riches of the world. Finally, those with hearts like good soil allowed the Word to take root and to grow, establish strong roots, and produce fruit.

The condition of people's hearts is a direct result of all the choices they have made throughout their lifetime. Each choice made turns people into something different than they were before making the choice. When I offered a Gift, there was no way that I could know in what condition that person's heart was. My Gift wouldn't do much of anything for the first three groups, but I was thankful when they took it because by making the choice to take the Gift and possibly read it, they just might cause a change that would bring their heart closer to good soil. The fourth group, those with hearts of good soil, were ready for God's Word.

I didn't know the condition of people's hearts by looking at them, but then that wasn't my job. I simply was to offer the Gift to everyone, and in the process, I would reach some with hearts of fertile soil. But God knew the condition of each heart. He knew those who deep down inside were tired of living a godless way of life and wanted to make a change. God led them to me, and I was able to offer them a life-changing Gift that would help them to turn from their sinful ways by accepting Jesus into their lives as their Lord and Savior.

Lesson Learned #6

It occurred to me that when I was sharing Jesus with someone, it could just be a random encounter, or it could be a divine appointment. God wants everyone to have everlasting life. He works in the lives of the unsaved and provides them with the opportunity to receive Jesus. To do this, there has to be someone who is willing to tell them about Jesus. God knows when a person is ready to accept Christ, and he provides the circumstances for the encounter to take place. In any case, I knew that when I approached people and gave them a Gift, I might never know the fruit that that encounter might bear, but I knew that the person I gave it to would be closer to God as a result of it. God is looking for faithful servants who will share the Good News, and when he finds one, he will work out the details providing the opportunities for that person to witness. Remember, some plant, some water, but God gives the growth.

I wanted to share the Good News of Jesus Christ with at least one person. More than one would be great, but I felt that if I found that one person and shared the Gospel with him or her that I would have accomplished my goal. There were many days when seemingly nothing happened. I say that from my point of view. I, of course, can't speak for the others in the equation. I learned early on that something always did happen even if I didn't see it. God was at work in this ministry, and people's lives were touched. If I didn't see it, so be it. God knew what was happening, and he was working in the lives of the people I approached. I just wanted him to use me for whatever His purpose was.

CHAPTER 7

Bus Stop Ministry

Trust in the Lord with all your heart, and do
not rely on your own insight. In all your ways
acknowledge him, and he will make straight
your paths.

—Proverbs 3:5–6

With my *Four Spiritual Laws* approach all worked out and
with my understanding that God would bring those who
needed to hear the Good News to me, once I had overcome all
the additional reasons why I shouldn't share the Good News,
I was ready to go out into the world and share the Good News
with whomever God put in my path.

I had chosen the Rosslyn Metro Train Station for my
distribution point to hand out my Gifts. It was only a few
minutes away from my workplace, and it seemed like a great
place to share the Good News of Jesus Christ by giving away
my Gifts. I could easily spend my lunch hour there.

As I write these words, I am able to see something that I

didn't at the time that all this was happening. God's hand was in all I was doing. I can see that God was leading me through this process in an amazing way. He knew that in my heart I wanted to tell the world about Jesus but didn't on my own know how. He took my willing spirit, a step at a time, at my pace, and led me to where I wanted to be. All one needs is the desire to spread the Good News, and God will make it happen in a most amazing way.

Along the way, I met face to face with hundreds of people—some of them only once for a few moments and others, more often. In part 2, I will be sharing my journal with you, which somewhat details the people I met while sitting on the bus stop bench at the Rosslyn Metro Train Station. But more about that later. In the next chapter, I want to share with you some of the people I met at the Rosslyn Metro Train Station who were very special to me and of whom I will always have fond and lasting memories.

CHAPTER 8

People I Met

People are guests in our story, the same way we
are guests in theirs. But we all meet each other
for a reason because every person is a personal
lesson waiting to be told.

—Lauren Klarfeld

There were a number of "regulars" at the Rosslyn Station.
They would just show up most every day and commune
with their peers. It was a community of sorts, and I had the
pleasure of meeting and getting to know lots of nice people.
Some of the people I met and came to know quite well were
Lois, Ginny Crouch, Dwight Moody, John (not his real name),
and Mary (not her real name).

Here is a brief introduction to each of them.

My Friend Lois

Right next to the Rosslyn Metro Station, there is a pastry/coffee shop called Tivoli's. I discovered this when I first started working at my job in Rosslyn. I would allow extra time each morning so I could stop for coffee and, on the rare occasion, a pastry after my long ride in on the metro. If I was early enough, I would find a seat at one of the few tables they had. Since there was a shortage of tables, it was a common practice to share a table with someone, even a total stranger, when there was an empty seat. This was how I met my lifelong friend Lois.

Lois was retired and about fifteen or twenty years older than I was. She was quite attractive and well dressed. You could tell by looking at her that she purchased only the finest clothing and took good care of it.

Lois was a very generous and friendly person and well known by most of the customers who frequented Tivoli's. She was well loved by all of the staff. She was also good friends with the manager, owner, and pastry chef.

I don't remember the exact way or day I met Lois, but it would have been early on, for we were friends for a long time. I am not even sure who made the first move, but it was probably Lois. She was quite outgoing and loved making new friends. I suspect she just came up to my table one day and asked if she could join me.

Our morning coffee soon became a regular thing, and I would see Lois almost every morning. We really enjoyed our morning coffee and conversation. Most of the time, we would discuss current events and the scandals of the day. Occasionally, I would learn something about the workers at Tivoli's. Sometimes others would join us, and I would meet someone new. Lois already knew them, of course, and made the introductions.

It wasn't long before Lois and I would occasionally have lunch together. We would meet at Tivoli's and then walk or metro to a restaurant nearby.

We really became close friends.

In her final years, Lois became quite ill. I would visit her apartment, and she was always quite glad to see me.

Lois and I didn't talk much about religion, but after I started Bus Stop Ministry, she would see me on occasion handing out Gifts. Then one day, we talked about what I was doing, and I gave her a Gift. I explained the Good News to her, and she prayed to receive Jesus as her Lord and Savior. What a blessing and relief.

After quite a bit of suffering, Lois passed away. I was quite happy that she had accepted Jesus. I am confident that she is now in heaven enjoying Jesus, in the company of the saints and the choirs of angels. If they have coffee and pastries in heaven, I am sure she is enjoying some every morning, chatting with all those there in her outgoing, friendly way.

Ginny

When I began sharing my Gifts at the metro station on my lunch hours, one of my big concerns was what if someone from my place of employment came by? What would I do? What would I say? It was easier to hand out Gifts to total strangers whom you may or may not ever see again, but what about handing out a Gift to someone at my workplace? What would my coworkers think? What would they say? What kind of reputation would I have as a result of it? It wasn't long before it happened.

One day, a group of employees from my company walked by, either on their way to lunch or returning back to work. I knew most of them. Well, this was going to be my test. What would I do? I know I talked to the Lord when it happened, but I am not sure what I said or what his answer was. In the end, I treated them just like anyone else walking by. I offered them a Gift.

It wasn't as bad as I thought it would be. Some of them took the Gift; others didn't. Some of them recognized me, and others didn't. Well, it was all over in a couple of minutes, and I learned that there is no difference whether you know the person or not. They all need Jesus, and those who didn't know him and received a Gift were well on their way.

Shortly thereafter, I received an email at work. It was from a young lady in the science department. Here's what it said:

> Mr. Whitford, I have an extraneous question for you, a question in which the chance that I am asking the wrong person is very great. A month or so ago, I was going out to lunch with some other people from the Science Division, and someone standing at the metro stop handed me a copy of the Gospel of John. Now, one of the folks I was with said, "He works at our company. I know him," and she told me your name. After trying once unsuccessfully to stop by your office, I finally figured the simplest thing would be to ask you directly whether you have spent your lunch hours that way or whether my friend just had you mixed up with somebody. If she was confused, then I am sorry to inconvenience you with this out-of-the-ordinary question. If not, thanks for the copy of John.

Wow! I was really blessed by this email. I sent her a reply and said I would like the pleasure of meeting her. Soon thereafter, I went over to the science department to find the young lady who had sent the email.

Her name was Ginny. Ginny worked at my company as a botanical research assistant at their international headquarters. She was well qualified for the positions with a Bachelor of Science in biology and a Bachelor of Arts in history from the College of William and Mary, Williamsburg. She also had a master's in forest ecology from Auburn University in Alabama.

Ginny was a lovely Christian young lady, and it was a wonderful meeting. We had a nice discussion about tracts, witnessing, and other Christians at our company. I really enjoyed meeting her. She had met the Lord about ten years earlier and was active in her church. We became great friends.

Once again, I was really blessed by the following email that I received from her after our visit:

> Did you tell me, last week, that you pray that everyone you give one of those little books will come to know the Lord through reading the Gospel of John? I thought, after we talked, that that is very interesting because I became a Christian through reading the Gospel of John about ten years ago.

Amazing! Surprised by God. One of the things about witnessing is that you have to take it on faith that you are fruitfully doing the Lord's work. It is a work that receives little positive feedback, but once in a while, the Lord lets you know that he is pleased with what you are doing and encourages you to continue on. To know that Ginny had received Jesus as a result of someone giving her a Gospel of John was a source of encouragement and made me realize that my labor was not in vain. I took it as an acknowledgment from my Heavenly Father that he was pleased with my work and I was richly blessed.

Unfortunately, Ginny's life was taken in a tragic fire at her home, a 250-year-old farmhouse in the Virginia mountains. It was a great loss for all who knew her and for the scientific community. I know that as you read this, she is basking in the presence of the Lord.

Ginny was a beautiful Christian young lady whose life was taken way before her time, and she will be greatly missed by all. I thank the Lord for the opportunity to meet and get to know Ginny.

Dwight Moody

One day while handing out Gifts, I met a man who told me his name was Dwight Moody. This set me back for a moment. I was quite familiar with the Moody Bible Institute in Chicago,

Illinois, and couldn't believe that I was talking to the founder. He was much older than I was, so I thought it was quite possible that it was him.

Dwight Moody, the founder of Moody Bible Institute, after completing the fifth grade, started out as a shoe salesman and set out into the world to make his way. He attended church at the YMCA and became a Christian at age eighteen. He had a burning desire to share Christ and did so through many crusades. He and his team would prepare for the crusade with house-to-house canvassing and worked with local churches. Many were saved. Mr. Moody realized that he needed an army of Christians to reach the unsaved. He started schools and summer camps, which finally became the Moody Bible Institute. He was a tireless preacher who preached six sermons a day.

Could this be the same Dwight Moody? Before actually meeting him, I had seen him on previous occasions sharing the Good News one-on-one with people around the metro station.

When we finally met and he told me his name, I couldn't believe my ears. After some discussion, I found out that he wasn't the Dwight Moody of the Moody Bible Institute. Apparently, his parents with the last name Moody decided to name him Dwight in honor of the great Dwight Moody.

Dwight was a real blessing to me. He was such a level-headed, calm, cool, and collected individual who loved the Lord. His love for Jesus just radiated off his face. We had many discussions about sharing Jesus, and I learned a great deal from Dwight. While I was quite happy to hand someone a Gift, Dwight convinced me that I needed to look for opportunities to talk to people and get to know them when possible.

At times, when you minister to the lost, it is easy to get down or discouraged when nothing seems to be happening—the dry times. But then someone like Dwight comes along, and just by being with him, you are refreshed and renewed and anxious to go out and share the Good News. Dwight had that effect on me.

John (Not His Real Name)

One of the first people I befriended at the Rosslyn Metro Train Station was John. John liked to come over to the metro station on his lunch hour and sit on the benches. It wasn't long before we noticed each other and started a conversation. John worked in Rosslyn. He liked to talk about the different military engagements that our country has been involved in.

This wasn't a problem at first. I enjoyed John and our conversations. However, after a while, it became an issue because he wanted to talk about war things, and I was there to share Jesus. With John sitting next to me, the spot for someone that I could share Jesus with was taken.

One day, it occurred to me that I should share Jesus with John. I asked John if he knew where he was going to go when he died. He said he didn't know. I gave him a Gift and used this opportunity to share the *Four Spiritual Laws* with him. He listened to my presentation. When I came to the part where I asked if he wanted to pray to receive Jesus Christ, John said yes. He prayed with me to receive Jesus as his personal Lord and Savior. That was wonderful, but after accepting Jesus, John went back to talking about the military.

John presented a big challenge for me in that he kept me from sharing the Good News. I really enjoyed our conversations, but I was there to share the Good News. How could I manage this without hurting John's feelings? After all, he had become a friend. It was my fault for not being honest with him. I had to figure out how to get back to doing what I was there to do. Finally, I figured it out. If John was there when I arrived, I would sit next to him as usual and have a conversation. When someone sat down next to me on the other side, I would politely excuse myself from our conversation, turn away from John, turn to the new arrival, and proceed with my approach.

There was an additional benefit to this approach. When I excused myself from my conversation with John to share the Good News with someone who had sat down next to me, John was able to hear the entire conversation, including my presentation of the Good News. I have no idea whether he was paying attention. I am sure he heard what I had to say.

John and I were friends for a couple of years. When my job situation changed, I was no longer able to spend my lunch hour at the Rosslyn Station, and I was unable to see John. I knew I would miss seeing him and having our conversations.

Mary (Not Her Real Name)

On February 25, 1992, I met a Spanish lady who knew my friend John. Her name was Mary. She desperately needed money. Somehow, she had lost her rent money and wouldn't say how. She was asking for eighty dollars. Mary was a very dramatic person. Each time I saw her, some devastating tragedy had occurred, and she was convinced that she would not be able to recover from it without my financial help. Mary was a Bible-bearing Christian who carried her Bible with her at all times. She belonged to an Assembly of God Church. Mary was surprised that I was a Catholic. I am not sure why. I asked her for the name of her church, but she didn't seem to know it or didn't want to tell me. I asked her if she had gone to them for help. She said she had not and told me it was because they were poor. I didn't have good feelings about this. It didn't seem that it was from the Lord, so I didn't give her the eighty dollars. I did buy her a twenty-dollar metro card to help her to get back and forth to work. Mary told me she wanted the cash so she could get a discount at the metro center. I told her it didn't matter about the discount. She accepted the card and took a Gift. I also gave her the Spanish version of the *Four Spiritual Laws*.

As I thought about Mary, the passage from Matthew 25:31–40 came to mind. Jesus had just come in glory, and he was praising the faithful brothers who fed the hungry, gave drink to the thirsty, clothed the naked, gave shelter to the homeless, and visited the sick and those in prison. The Bible doesn't say anything about questioning their motives. Then he says, "Truly, I say to you, as you did it to one of the least of these my brethren, you did it to me" (Matthew 25:40). In this situation, I interpreted scripture to mean that by helping Mary, I was helping Jesus.

Mary was certainly a needy person. Would the eighty dollars have given her shelter for another month? Would I have done this for Jesus?

A couple of days later, I saw Mary again. This time, she needed money for her phone bill. She cleaned houses and relied on her phone for work. I gave her seventy dollars. I decided to count it as a deposit in my heavenly account. Mary was very needy, and I came to doubt the veracity of her requests. I really wanted to help, but it was hard to do—to trust her. She professed Jesus as Lord and was in need. I asked God to prevent it from happening if it was not to be. I know there are lessons in this for me. Mary helped me to hand out Gifts. She asked for more when she ran out.

The next time I saw Mary, she wanted to go back to her country and wanted help getting there. I told her I couldn't help her.

Each time I saw Mary, she had some kind of a financial need that she wanted me to meet.

- Thursday, April 9, 1992—Mary needed bus fare to get home.
- Monday, April 27, 1992—Mary had worked for a lady who went away on a trip without paying her, and she didn't have enough for the rent.
- Wednesday, June 17, 1992—Mary was sick. I bought her some Tylenol and lunch. She wanted help getting into an apartment. I said I wouldn't be able to help her with that.
- Wednesday, July 29, 1992—Mary was there, and I spent most of the time discussing her problems. She was very thankful.
- Thursday, August 6, 1992—I spent most of my time discussing Mary's rent deposit problem.
- Monday, August 17, 1992—I spent the whole time with Mary. She didn't want to fill out the form for

immigration because she said she already had. She wanted help with a deposit. I didn't help her.

- Thursday, September 24, 1992—Yesterday, Mary told me she was robbed and needed money for rent. I discussed this with my wife. We agreed that our main concern was that she would keep coming back for more. I felt we should give her the money and let her know the well had run dry. In seeking the Lord, he told me to verify the robbery. In any case, Mary didn't show up the next day, so I was unable to give her the money for rent.
- Thursday, November 19, 1992—I saw Mary today. She wants a computer for her daughter.
- Thursday, December 3, 1992—Mary came today, and I spent most of my time talking with her about her current situation.
- Thursday, December 10, 1992—I saw Mary at the metro station. We talked about her current situation.

Overall, Mary was a very needy person and difficult to work with. She had lots of needs and was constantly searching for someone to meet those needs. She presented a huge challenge to me. I wanted to be sensitive and sympathetic to her constant needs. Jesus tells us to help out the less fortunate, but Mary was beyond the scope of Bus Stop Ministry. I sincerely believe that Mary loved the Lord, but she needed a professional (pastor or social worker) to help her get her life straightened out. Mary would have been much better off if I had been able to help her get the proper help, but giving her money to solve the new problem that surfaced each time I met her was not the answer.

When my current job situation changed, I was no longer able to spend my lunch hour at the Rosslyn Metro Train Station, and I lost track of Mary and haven't seen her since then.

Lesson Learned #12

You will encounter people that have deep seeded problems which will be beyond your scope to deal with and solve. Develop a list of pastors, social workers and others that are trained to handle these kinds of issues. Then when you encounter someone who needs help, you can refer them to an appropriate resource.

PART 2

My Journal

And now, go, write it before them on a tablet, and inscribe it in a book, that it may be for the time to come as a witness for ever.

—Isaiah 30:8

In the following chapters, I will share my selected journal entries for the first two years of Bus Stop Ministry. I must forewarn you that I am not great at writing journal entries. Each time I made an entry, I could remember the next day exactly what I was thinking about as I wrote the entry, even though I may have left out some details. Years later, it was a great deal more difficult to decipher. Any omitted details are gone from my memory, and all that is left is the entry I wrote. Had I known at the time that I would be sharing my journal entries in a book, I would have been much more diligent about details. If you find you are confused by something I say in an entry or if you realize you have heard this before, don't spend too much time on it. Just go on to the next entry. But it is what it is, and I think anyone seriously interested in witnessing will benefit from it.

Starting a conversation about Jesus with a total stranger is exciting and produces some amazing results. For those who oppose what you are telling them, you are bringing the issue up to them once again. Even if they reject it, they are forced to revisit the issue and possibly see the folly of their ways. Those who say yes when you ask them if they would like to pray to accept Jesus as their Lord and Savior result in a total blessing. Even conversation with those who don't accept Jesus is quite rewarding because you know that they will at least think about something they may have buried years ago. They may even read the Gospel of John that you have given them and come closer to conversion. I know I enjoy reading the journal and the memories it brings back to me. I hope you will too.

I recorded an entry about every conversation when something unusual happened and when I learned something significant. I also recorded entries on days when nothing at all happened, but I have filtered out these entries from the journal I am sharing with you. It was just for the record that I went out that day. I took what was left and selected entries that I thought were more significant and have included them here. Along the way, I learned many lessons, and I have already shared some of them with you in previous chapters. In part 2, I will share more of them with you as they occur. I am including them because I think they will be helpful for those of you who will go out and share the Good News. I call these Lessons Learned. There are forty-two lessons learned altogether. They are, for the most part, observations I made as I handed out the Gifts. While standing at a metro station, giving out Gifts, my mind was always racing, trying to figure out what was going on, how I was being received, and if I needed to do anything more or different. These Lessons Learned are interspersed throughout the text, as I learned them, but I am also including a complete list in Appendix A.

Every day I went to work, except when I had a doctor's appointment, was at a seminar, or got tied up at the office, I went over to the Rosslyn Metro Train Station at lunchtime with great hopes of having an opportunity of sharing Jesus.

There were many days when I gave out Gifts and nothing happened—at least from what I could see. God only knows what transpired when someone was presented with the Good News of Jesus Christ and how the Gospel of John touched their heart. But I faithfully carried out my job, which was to hand out my Gifts. God's job was to use them in whatever way he wanted to for those who received them. What happened to my Gift after I gave it away, no one but God knows. What matters is that He used them for his purpose—just like the many Gospel of John booklets my grandmother gave me. She was faithful in giving them to me. Sometimes I would read from them, and I know they contributed to my making a decision to follow the Lord.

On other days, something remarkable would occur. It was these days I lived for. They raised my excitement and joy to great levels. They were a confirmation that I was called to this ministry and that God was actively involved in Bus Stop Ministry.

Once I took the initial step and started sharing the Good News, things began to fall into place. I felt much more comfortable and confident as time went on. It was actually kind of exciting. On any given day, I was ready for an adventure. I had no idea what I would face or how I would have to modify my approach, but it was exciting, and something to look forward to.

On the days when nothing unusual happened, it was a bit discouraging. On these days, Satan was right there trying to convince me that I should just give it up. After all, I wasn't doing anything good, he would say. He didn't want me to share my faith. His job was to beat me down and discourage me from doing that, but I knew deep down in my heart that he wasn't going to be able to stop me.

Yes, there were the dry times, but the most amazing experiences in my life occurred when I told someone about

Jesus and that person accepted him as Lord and Savior. I could almost hear the angels in heaven rejoicing. I can't explain the joy I experienced when that happened, especially the first time. After seventeen years, I was finally able to take the love of Jesus within me and give it away. It was amazing. This is what we are all called to do. This is the great commission given to us by Jesus.

For each person I approached, I came with a message of hope. The book of Ephesians tells us that before knowing Jesus, "you were at that time separated from Christ, alienated from the commonwealth of Israel, and strangers to the covenants of promise, having no hope and without God in the world" (Ephesians 2:12). A hopeless person is one who is beaten down by Satan and can see no way out of the situation. My message for those people was that there is a way out and that way is the Lord Jesus Christ. It was a blessing for me to approach someone who was lost and searching for a way out and to tell him or her that Jesus is the way. People would light up with hope because they found what they were searching for—Jesus.

Our Heavenly Father is in charge, and I believe that he used each one of the Gifts that I handed out for his purpose. I believe he answered the prayer I prayed each day as I made my way over to the Rosslyn Metro Train Station that each person who received a Gift would come to know Jesus. I am a firm believer in answered prayer. However, once the Gift left my hands, I had no idea of how God would use it to minister to the person who received it. I was just glad to be an instrument he used for his purpose.

Not knowing how effective my ministry was was all right with me. My overall goal was to be instrumental in one person's conversion. Were that to happen, I would consider the ministry a huge success.

I have included in Appendix B a Gift count. It is a spreadsheet showing the location and how many Gifts I gave out for each day I went out for those two years.

Two years of handing out Gifts at the Rosslyn Metro Train Station was a great experience for me. I met hundreds of people from all walks of life and had the pleasure of telling them about Jesus. The purpose of this book is to pass on what I learned to you, the reader, in hopes that it will help you and encourage you to go out and witness. My prayer is that God will richly bless you with these journal entries and they will encourage you to go and share Jesus with others.

CHAPTER 9

Year One

So it is not the will of my Father who is in heaven
that one of these little ones should perish.

—Matthew 18:14

Wednesday, January 2, 1991

I gave Gifts to people waiting for a bus and some to others
inside the Rosslyn Metro Train Station. One lady on the
escalator said, "Wait a minute. I have something for you."
It was a booklet published by the Seventh Day Adventists
entitled *Steps to Christ*. It included a form to be completed
and mailed in for a free Bible study course.

> ### Lesson Learned #9
>
> I discovered that when you openly share your faith with others, they often will open up about theirs. Sometimes they even share that they don't have any faith and why.

I boarded my bus and gave a Gift to the bus driver. He took it and thanked me. I realized that for the most part, I wouldn't see those I gave a Gift to again, but in the case of the bus driver and my barber, I knew I would see them again. I decided that when I saw them again, I wouldn't say anything about the Gift but would be ready to answer any questions or enter into a discussion if they so desired.

Thursday, January 3, 1991

It just so happened that I saw the same bus driver again. He made no indication that I had given him a Gift.

I gave away six Gifts on the way to work. One lady asked if it was in Spanish. I said, "No," but began to think I should probably get a Spanish version.

I gave away six Gifts at lunchtime. About half of the people I offered a Gift to said no, especially the well-dressed, white-collar workers. It seemed to me that blue-collar workers were more apt to take the Gift.

Lesson Learned #10

I came to the conclusion that when people say no or refuse the Gift, it isn't necessarily because it is a Christian Bible book. For the most part, when I approach people offering them a free Gift, they have no idea what it is. A lot of people subscribe to the adage that there is no such thing as a free lunch (gift), and there is always a catch, requiring something from you that makes the free gift not so free. I could have been a salesman selling timeshares for all they knew. In any case, I concluded that I shouldn't think that they were rejecting the Gift but that they just didn't believe that it was really free and didn't want to be bothered.

Friday, January 4, 1991

At lunchtime, I went over to the Rosslyn Metro Train Station. On my way over, I prayed I would be successful. I asked the Lord to bring the people who would benefit from the Gift to me. I wanted to do my part—to be a willing vessel for the Lord.

Instead of moving around approaching people, I stood near the entrance to the station. There were a lot of people just standing around waiting, and this gave me a chance to strike up a conversation. Many refused the Gift, but others thanked me.

One lady was so pleased to get the Gift that she came back once she realized what it was and offered me $1.00. I refused it, and we began a conversation. I asked her if she was a Christian. She said that most Christian organizations would say she was because she believed God could be found in other religions. She then went on to say that she believed Jesus was the Son of God. She was pleasant to talk to and went away reading her Gift.

Another lady said she preferred another Gospel. I think it was the Gospel of Mark. She also wanted to know what version of the Bible it was and which group I represented. I told her I didn't represent a group but was handing them out on my own. She took the Gift.

I prayed, as had become my habit after giving out Gifts, that all who had received a Gift would read it and come to know Jesus.

Monday, January 7, 1991

We had a lot of snow today, and the government workers were dismissed early. I handed out twelve Gifts at the Rosslyn Metro Train Station. It seemed to me that there were a lot of rejections. I suspect it was because of the snow and metro riders' preoccupation with getting home. I made a decision to only offer to people who were alone. Offering to a group was problematic since it introduced a peer pressure aspect.

Lesson Learned #11

I observed that when there was a group, people were less likely to accept the Gift because of the presence of the others. They also might react in a negative or smart-alecky manner, so it would be better to avoid groups.

Tuesday, January 8, 1991

It was really cold, and I had the thought that I was being foolish for not getting in out of the cold. But then I thought that it is okay to be a fool for Christ.

I was starting to wonder what would happen and how I would act if someone from my company came by. Would I offer him or her a Gift? What would he or she think of me standing out in the cold giving out Bible books?

Saturday, January 19, 1991

I gave out Gifts at Bob's Big Boy restaurant after having breakfast with someone from the prayer group. One lady refused the Gift because she was a Christian. I didn't know what to say. A man told me that he liked tracts like the Gift, and since he was already a Christian, he would give it away to someone else. He asked me what church I belonged to, and I told him St Mary's. He said, "Oh."

I gave Gifts to five or six men who had been together at Bob's Restaurant and had been praying. They each took it without a word. One man said, "Praise the Lord!" when I gave him the Gift.

Tuesday, January 29, 1991

One lady asked for two Gifts and offered to give me a contribution. I was pretty sure she had someone in mind that she felt needed to hear the message and this would be a good way of delivering it. Praise the Lord. What a pleasure it was helping someone who wanted to share the Good News. She had crutches and was holding a boy. I wasn't sure I should give her one because I didn't know how she could take it without falling. We took it slow, and it worked out okay. I gave her two Gifts without taking the contribution.

Wednesday, January 30, 1991

One man said, "What is this?" when I offered the Gift. I answered, "It is a free Gift." He looked at it, and he gave me a definite "No!" These are the folks I am really concerned about. They are offered the Good News, and after clarifying what is being offered, they reject it. I need to pray that God will remove the scales from their eyes.

Wednesday, February 6, 1991

One of the metro Train Station workers came up to me, and I offered him a Gift. He said he already had one and then went on to encourage me in what I was doing—getting out the Word of God. He wanted to say more, but he was distracted by a customer who came up to ask him something.

A lady came back after receiving a Gift to ask me how she could get the program *In Touch* on the radio. I told her to tune in to 95.1 FM.

A good Christian friend in data entry saw the Gospel of John on my desk. I told her what I was doing with them, and I gave her one.

One lady took the Gift I offered her and then came back to return it to me and said she would only throw it away. I should have used this opportunity to try to enter into a conversation with her about why she felt that way. Many people just throw the Gift into the trash can as soon as they realize what it is, but she came back to tell me about it, and I missed the opportunity to talk with her about it.

Another lady also gave the Gift back to me. She said she was involved in a ministry that hands out tracts and that I should give it to someone else. Another missed opportunity. I should have asked her to keep it and give it to someone she knew.

Lesson Learned #13

Keep your ears open and listen to what people say to you. Most won't come up and ask you to tell them about the Good News. They will come back with questions or comments that you need to be able to interpret and use as a lead-in to the Good News message.

Lesson Learned #14

I noticed that if the first person in a queue heading for or exiting out of the metro said no when I offered the Gift, then the rest of the people in the group would most likely say no. If the first one of a group took the Gift, then the rest of the group would most likely take the Gift as well. They didn't want to miss out on the free something that the person before them received.

Friday, February 8, 1991

An Asian woman who didn't speak English very well asked me about Armageddon—she wanted to know where you could find it in the Bible. I told her it was near the end of the book of Revelation. I think she understood me.

Lesson Learned #15

It is essential to have a Bible with you in a ministry like this. People will ask you questions that can only be answered from scripture. The best way to answer their questions is to open up the Bible to the relevant chapter and verse and then let them read it. Also, if you don't know the answer or the scripture location, tell them that and that you will research it and get back to them. Try to set up a time and place to meet.

Friday, February 22, 1991

One young lady said, "Praise the Lord!" when she looked at her Gift and realized what it was. Then she came back and asked if she could have another one for a friend, which I gave her.

Tuesday, February 26, 1991

One man asked what it was, and when I told him, he kissed it. Shortly thereafter, someone hit the fare machine really hard and made a loud noise. I looked over, and it could have been the same man.

Wednesday, February 27, 1991

A metro policewoman approached me and asked what I was handing out. I showed her and offered her one. She said no and that I must be sure to not force anyone to take one. I said I wouldn't. She was quite nice.

Tuesday, March 5, 1991

One man said, "I am already saved. You can give it to someone else."

Lesson Learned #16

When people say that they are already a Christian and that I should give the Gift to someone else, it creates a great opportunity to offer the option for them to give it to someone else. I can say something like, "You are a Christian—great! Do you know someone who isn't a Christian and might benefit from it?" Take the opportunity to encourage others to reach out to the unsaved they know. This gives them a great way to witness to them. All Christians are called to witness, but some find it hard to do. By offering this challenge, it gives them an opportunity.

Monday, March 11, 1991

One man took the Gift and said, "Free?" I said yes, and he continued on his way.

Another young man stopped and asked me which church I was from. I told him I was a Christian and that I attended the Catholic church. He was a Jehovah's Witness. We both agreed that the Word must get out.

Lesson Learned #17

When meeting people of other faiths and denominations, the best approach is to just share my Christian faith and to follow the leading of the Holy Spirit.

Friday, March 15, 1991

A metro employee approached me and said, "You can't distribute that here (inside the station)," and that I would have to go out to the street. I chose not to be confrontational and went outside the metro station.

Lesson Learned #18

The best approach to dealing with metro employees is to respect them and do what they say. They are only doing their job. Each employee is different. Some don't really care whether you distribute information, and others don't seem to want you to do it. For the latter, I don't know if it is because they don't like what you are distributing or if it is because metro has some sort of policy regarding distribution. In any case, I made a conscious decision not to be confrontational with them.

Later on, as I was walking down the street, heading for home, a car pulled up at the curb. A young lady got out and gave me an invitation to visit the Mormon Temple. I called it a church, and she corrected me calling it a temple. I asked her if they let people in the temple now, and she said no, but they had chapels. I gave her a Gift, and she thanked me.

Tuesday, March 26, 1991

One young lady who didn't take the Gift told me, "You get an A for effort." That was very nice, but I would rather that she had taken the Gift.

Thursday, March 28, 1991

One young lady said, "I am already a Christian. You can save it for someone else." This was another missed opportunity. I should have asked her to give it to someone she knew who could use it, but I didn't.

One man was with a friend. I gave a Gift to the man, and his friend came back and asked me for one. Later, I saw him reading it on a bench. I should have asked him if he had any questions. Giving out Gifts was a great way to share the Good News, but I needed to find opportunities to share on a one-on-one basis.

Lesson Learned #19

Opportunities to share one-on-one happen very quickly, and you have to be ready when the opportunity arises.

Friday, March 29, 1991, Good Friday

I shared Jesus with a young man from Bolivia. He shared with me that he had been hassled by a Jehovah's Witness. He said he is Catholic and that he doesn't go to church. I encouraged him to go. I told him that God loved him and wanted to have fellowship with him. He left when his bus came. I should have shared the *Four Spiritual Laws* with him. I was very excited about having the opportunity to share God's love with him.

Monday, April 8, 1991

I gave a Gift to a bus driver who was waiting to start his shift. He studiously read it while I was passing out my other Gifts. After he read it, before he left to start his shift, he said, "God bless you." He gave me a copy of a tract that he used to witness. I didn't ask, but after talking to him, I wondered if he witnessed on his job while driving the bus. I have seen many bus drivers who talk to the regulars as they work. What a wonderful opportunity to witness.

Tuesday, April 9, 1991

I met a man named Dwight Moody. I shared more about him in an earlier chapter. As we talked, I could see that he had a great love for the Lord. He goes about sharing the Good News with all who will listen and has been all over the world. He likes to take his time and get to know a person before he tells them the Good News and gives them the opportunity to invite Jesus into their life as Lord and Savior.

What a joy it was to meet a man with a passion for lost souls and for getting the Word of God out.

Thursday, April 11, 1991

I gave the first Gift to a man who came back and introduced himself. He attended Clarendon Baptist Church. He shook my hand and said it was a good thing I was doing. He was a nice young man.

I gave a Gift to a Metro worker who goes to a full Gospel church in Maryland. His pastor preaches the full sixty-six books of the Bible. He likes the King James Version of the Bible but said he would read the Gift, which is the New King James version.

Friday, April 19, 1991, My Birthday

I am and always have been a person who loves his birthday. It's the very best day of the year. Maybe I am this way because my mother was convinced that a person's birthday was the best day of the year for him or her. She always made me and my two brothers' birthdays very special occasions. My mom was always fair. She was careful to give each one of her three sons the same amount of love and attention. On our birthday, she would focus totally on the birthday boy. We were given our favorite dinner and best of all a cake of our choosing. It was wonderful.

So, when my birthday came, it was just like any other, and I wanted it to be something special. Ahead of time I placed an order for John's Gospels. I celebrated by taking the day off from work. I loaded up my backpack with the box of Gifts (408 Gospels of John) and set off for downtown Washington DC to give them away. I also had a 100 *Four Spiritual Laws*.

My first stop was Lafayette Park. It is right across from the White House. I had decided that it was where I wanted to start distribution. When I reached the park, it was time to hand out Gifts. A homeless man came up to me. I greeted him, and he in return asked me for money for food. This didn't surprise me. It's what happens most times when I encounter a homeless person. He had long, unruly, and dirty blond hair and a long beard to match. He looked very much like I would imagine John the Baptist looked. He wasn't clothed with camel's hair, nor did he have a leather girdle around his waist, and I don't know that he ate locusts and wild honey. He spoke with a German accent. I told him I had no money for him but offered him a Gift. He wouldn't take it. He said he knew more about the Gospel of John than I did. We talked a bit. He was from Germany and had been traveling around

America. There was a moment of silence, and then he asked me if I knew the Holy Spirit was a person. I thought this was a rather unusual question for a homeless man to ask and wondered what exactly he was up to. I responded by saying, "Yes," that he was one of the three persons in the Trinity. I told him that Jesus died for us and was risen defeating death and now sits at the right hand of God the Father. I told him that when we accept Jesus as Lord and Savior, he sends the Holy Spirit to empower us for ministry. He nodded in agreement and then proceeded to tell me that he was the Holy Spirit! This really set me back. I never thought I would encounter the Holy Spirit face to face in my ministry and wasn't sure how to respond. It was the last thing I expected to hear from him. But then could it possibly be true? Could this really be the Holy Spirit? I searched my mind for scriptures that would confirm or deny this and came up empty handed.

As I recovered from my shock, he asked me if I could see his glow. I looked closely but didn't really see a glow, so I responded, "No." I think he was somewhat set back by my response.

At this point, he changed the subject and asked me again for a dollar for food. I said no, but that if he was hungry, I would buy him a sandwich. He said he was hungry. There was a Hardy's nearby, so we went there.

I bought him a bacon cheeseburger, large fries, and a large coffee. He got a table. I brought his food to him and told him I was going back to the park to hand out my Gifts. He seemed shocked that I would leave the Holy Spirit in a fast-food restaurant.

I went back to Lafayette Park and stood at the edge of the park facing the White House and Executive Office Building.

I met a husband and wife from Boston. He was a Christian and really encouraged about what I was doing. He said he was going to tell his church about me and that they would pray for me. I was quite moved by this and thanked them.

I gave Gifts to a couple busloads of kids. They all were eager to get one. One group, with the adult chaperones leading, said, "No," so the girls following said, "No," but the boys following the girls all said, "Yes."

One guy said he was a Catholic. I am not sure why that made a difference. Catholics read the Gospel of John too. I told him I was also Catholic.

Another guy, seemed like a wise guy, said he was a Jew. I told him it was for the Jews as well. He then said he was something else. I told him that it was a Gift for everyone.

I continued to hand out Gifts. I gave a Gift to a homeless man, and when he read the title (*Bread of Life*), he told me that he was the Bread of Life. I said to myself, "Oh no, not another one!"

I went to McDonald's for lunch and had some French fries, a cup of coffee, and a rest. After lunch, I walked over to McPherson Square Metro Train Station and handed out Gifts and *Four Spiritual Laws* at the top of the escalator. People seemed to be quicker to take the *Four Spiritual Laws* than the Gifts. One man came back and told me he had trouble with drinking. He had a wife and baby, but he kept giving in to temptation. I asked if he belonged to a church. He said no. I suggested he search out a church to belong to and seek help from the brothers and sisters for his drinking problems on a more committed basis. He seemed to understand. I should have offered to pray with him. I will pray for him.

I gave a young man from Georgia a dollar for bus fare to Olney. I bought a $2.55 metro ticket for another young man who needed to get to Vienna. It seemed to be my day for helping people who needed bus fare.

Soon the day was over, and it was time to go home for the wonderful birthday dinner my wife would prepare for me. Of course, this included a fabulous strawberry birthday cake as well.

Lesson Learned #20

I seem to be facing more situations where people open up to me with their issues and problems. I see this as a great opportunity to pray with them. It takes some courage to offer prayer to someone you don't know and have just met, but it can be very rewarding for all those who say yes. If people don't feel comfortable praying with a stranger, that is okay too. It's really up to them and how the Holy Spirit is working in their life.

Tuesday, April 23, 1991

I met a woman who is a Christian and felt she shouldn't take the Gift. I suggested that she take it and give it to someone else. She kept the Gift and said she was encouraged by what I was doing.

I met a man who is a student at a Washington area theological seminary where he is studying the Gospel of John and the books between the Old and New Testament. He wanted to know if I was going to give away any other books of the Bible. I told him I wasn't planning on it.

Monday, April 29, 1991

One young lady said to me, "If you continue in my word, you are truly my disciples, and you will know the truth, and the truth will make you free" (John 8:31–32). I should have known what it was but had to look it up. I am not sure what she meant, but most likely she meant that if those who take a Gift read it, then they will be set free.

Wednesday, May 15, 1991

While handing out my last few Gifts, I got into a discussion with an elderly man. I had seen him before and offered him a Gift, but he turned it down and said his eyes were bad so he couldn't read it anyway. Well, today as I handed out my last Gift, he said he would like one. I told him I had just given my last one away and that I would give him one next time I saw him.

Friday, May 17, 1991

I saw the elderly man again from the other day and gave him a Gift.

I went over to Gallery Place Metro Train Station and handed out about seventy-five *Four Spiritual Laws*. Two boys were selling papers. I gave them a *Four Spiritual Laws*, and then they started to hand them out. They went down the escalator and picked up the ones people had discarded and handed them out.

Gallery Place is a small station and wasn't very busy. It was about 5:30 p.m. If it had been thirty minutes earlier, it probably would have been much busier.

I went home to the Rockville Metro Train Station. While I was waiting for my daughter to pick me up, I handed out about twenty *Four Spiritual Laws*. Most people were receptive. It was a great opportunity and a good use of my time while I waited to be picked up. The *Four Spiritual Laws* is really meant to be used as a tool to lead someone to the Lord, but it is quite effective as a stand-alone.

Thursday, May 23, 1991

I gave a Gift to a young man whom I think I had given one before. He said he had read it. He seemed to want to talk, but his bus came. If I see him again, I will try to start up a conversation.

I mentioned this earlier, but ministering to this young man confirmed my premise that people waiting for a bus provides a great opportunity to witness. They have nothing to do but wait for their bus to arrive. Some make themselves busy, but for the most part, they are not really doing anything but waiting.

Friday, May 24, 1991

I went to the Foggy Bottom Metro Train Station. A man was panhandling at the top of the escalator approaching people coming up. I started handing out tracts to those going down the escalator. He got upset with me. I said he was facing those coming up, and I was giving to those going down. I asked him if I should leave, and he said no and left. I continued home, stopping at the Metro Center Train Station, where I gave out some *Four Spiritual Laws*.

Tuesday, May 28, 1991

The first person I met was a bus driver who attends Washington Bible College. He is a real source of encouragement. Through him, the Lord gave me the message, "What you are doing is not in vain." I really enjoy swapping testimonies with him and quoting scripture. He came to the Lord in 1984. He is from North Carolina—a real "country boy."

Friday, May 31, 1991

I gave away thirty *Four Spiritual Laws*. I went to the Clarendon Metro Train Station and handed out fifteen of the *Four Spiritual Laws*. Then on the way home, I handed out another fifteen at the Rockville Station.

While waiting for my wife, I met a young man who asked what I was handing out and wanted to know what my religion was. I told him I was Catholic. He told me he was a Baptist.

He is living in a rented room in Rockville. I think he wanted to talk, but my wife came. I should have asked him for his phone number so we could talk more. I hope to see him again.

Lesson Learned #21

There is a great temptation to keep in contact with some I meet. I don't think it is prudent to give out my phone number to a total stranger, but it might be okay to give out my email. An even better idea would be to set up a special email for Bus Stop Ministry. If people really want to stay in contact, then have them give you their phone or email.

Lesson Learned #22

After a few months, I began to see and offer Gifts to the same people. Even though I went to different metro stations, if I got there at about the same time I had been there before, chances were that I would see some of the same people. There is really no way to remember them all, but if they indicate that they already have received a Gift, then it is a great opportunity to get them into a conversation by asking if they read it or what they thought of it.

Those who have already said no may seem annoyed. However, if they say anything, it gives me a chance to discuss it with them. The key is to listen closely to the Holy Spirit and allow him to guide you.

Wednesday, June 5, 1991

I gave a Gift to a man who works where I work. He is really a funny guy. I think he missed his calling. He could have been a great comedian. I told him that there would be a quiz.

Lesson Learned #23

I am much more comfortable now with giving Gifts to people who work where I do than I was before. At first, I was worried about what they might think. Now it doesn't really matter to me. In my experience coworkers are a bit more receptive than most. When they notice me, they usually approach me. Also, it sets up an opportunity for me. If they ever have any questions or want to talk, they now know they can find me.

Saturday, June 8, 1991, God Bless America Rally, Downtown DC

I usually don't work on Saturdays, so I don't get on the metro Train System, but there was this great gathering of people who came to the God Bless America Rally in Downtown DC.

I gave away two thousand "Come Home, America" flyers with my friend's church. The number of people pouring out of the Federal Triangle Metro Train Station was awesome. They were all eager to receive. I just said, "God Bless America," and they would take a flyer. I think some may have thought that I was giving them a parade program. I had a lot of fun.

Thursday, June 13, 1991

I gave a man a Gift, and he asked me if I know where he could get some work. He was from North Carolina. I asked him why he left North Carolina, and he said his stepmother was mad at him. I think he missed her and was upset because she was mad at him. He hadn't eaten for two days, so I took him to Hardy's and got him a cheeseburger, fries, and a Coke.

Friday, June 14, 1991

I gave away Gifts at the Foggy Bottom Metro Train Station. I handed them out as people were entering the escalator to take them down to the Metro. After I finished, I went down and found twenty-seven *Four Spiritual Laws* in the trash. I hope that the others who took them keep them and read them or at least give them to someone else.

Lesson Learned #24

It's impossible to know what people do with the Gifts I give them. They may trash them, put them away, or—I hope—read them. If they do read them, what will they do next? Again, it is not for me to know.

My grandmother gave me copies of the Gospel of John. I just put them in my dresser drawer. I looked at them from time to time, and I truly believe that the message I found there had a large part in my conversion to Christianity.

I continue to pray that all who receive the Gifts will read them and come to know Jesus, but that is up to them. I continue to pray and believe that the Holy Spirit is working in each of them and that simply by my handing them out, whether they read or toss them, God is using me as his instrument to spread the Good News. Remember that "*Paul* planted, Apollos watered, but God gave the growth. So neither he who plants nor he who waters will see anything, but only God who gives the growth" (1 Corinthians 3:6–7).

Wednesday, June 26, 1991

After I finished handing out the Gifts, I purchased a coffee and sat down next to a lady who was waiting for a bus and reading the Gift I had given her. I hoped this might be my chance to lead someone to the Lord. I tried to talk to her, but she seemed hesitant. I backed off and waited for some indication that she might like to talk, but her bus came, and she left.

Saturday, June 29, 1991

I met a young man who seemed to be spaced out, but after talking to him for a while, I thought he seemed rational. He said he was a Christian. He had many questions. I should have asked him when and how he became a Christian. I decided that I should always carry a *Four Spiritual Laws* with me to use in instances like this.

Lesson Learned #25

When people share their faith with you, pause and take the time to let them tell their story. Get to know them. Make as many friends in Christ as you can. Establishing a relationship with them may provide an opportunity to pray for their needs or have them pray for yours.

Monday, July 8, 1991

I met an elderly lady who asked about the Gift. I told her it was the Gospel of John. She opened it and saw Billy Graham (on the copyright page). She said she gives to his ministry. We discussed him. She asked for another Gift to give to her friend.

Lesson Learned #26

Observation: Since the beginning of Bus Stop Ministry, it seems that mostly blue-collar workers and minorities are interested in what I am offering. Young, upscale professionals seem to reject my offering. I don't even think that most of them know what I am offering; they just reject it. I am not sure what this means. It is just something I have observed.

Friday, July 19, 1991

I gave away a hundred *Four Spiritual Laws* at the Silver Spring Metro Train Station. Two people took one, stopped, and read it and insisted that I take them back. So I did.

There were two Montgomery County policemen talking to a flower vendor. I don't know if he was doing something illegal or not. One of them came marching over to me and took a *Four Spiritual Laws* without saying anything. He glanced at it and then went back to his motorcycle and put it in the trunk. Most people were happy to take one.

Thursday, July 25, 1991

I was kind of in a hurry. I had just given a Gift to a lady and started to hand out to those sitting at the bus stop when the lady gave it back to me. I walked down the row of seats, and then when I came back, two or three gave them back as well. This is the first time it happened like this. I think it was the monkey see, monkey do effect. Very interesting. (This may have been a variation of **Lesson Learned #14**—Queuing Theory.)

Friday, July 26, 1991

I met a young woman who at first took a Gift and then returned it. She said she was a Christian and wanted me to give it to someone else. After handing out my Gifts, I went for coffee at Tivoli's, and she was there eating lunch. I sat at her table. She is in seminary at Princeton. She will graduate next year. She temps during the summer. She was at the church's general assembly. We discussed the controversial report on sexuality. She was glad things went on the way they did but also was glad that all the discussion took place.

In the spring of next year, she will send her résumé to the general assembly. Churches send requests for ministers there as well, and they are matched up. If a church is interested in a minister, they will contact the person. Ordination comes only after being accepted by a church, not at graduation. She was a very pleasant person. I suspect she will do very well in the ministry.

I gave out *Four Spiritual Laws* at McPherson Square Metro Train Station. One lady asked where she could get some of the booklets. She had been reading a book about witnessing and wanted to get some. I gave her the Campus Crusade 800 number and about twenty-five extras I had with me.

Wednesday, July 31, 1991

I saw Dwight Moody. We discussed how he uses tracts in his ministry. He tries to develop a relationship with the people to whom he ministers. That way, he can be more successful in leading them to the Lord. Since personal witnessing is what I want to do, I will give this a try. I went for coffee at Tivoli's and sat down at my favorite table. A man joined me—an editor for a magazine on oceans. I had a nice conversation with him and gave him a Gift. We didn't talk about it. He said, "Thanks."

Thursday, August 1, 1991

After handing out my eighteen Gifts, I went and sat down on the bus stop bench next to a man I have seen numerous times. I chatted with him. I gave him a Gift, and he thanked me. We didn't discuss it.

The trouble I am having is how to get the conversation going when I give someone a Gift. Am I going to be able to do this? Or is it my personality that keeps me from it? I don't think it is the fear of rejection, but maybe it is. Help me, Lord, to do this. Help me to understand. Help me to speak out in boldness. Help me to identify why I am having a problem with this. In Jesus's name, I pray. Amen.

Tuesday, August 6, 1991

I saw Dwight again. I observed him sharing the gospel with a woman. I talked with him about how to share the gospel. I told him I was a Catholic. Not much of a reaction from him, but I didn't think there would be.

I gave a Gift to a woman who works in data entry at my company.

Thursday, August 8, 1991

Most people seemed negative. Maybe it was me. One woman said she had seven of the Gifts at home that she would sell back to me. I think she was serious. This confirmed my theory that over time I was passing out the Gift to the same people and that some were taking them. I am still okay with that, but hopefully, they will give their extra Gifts to someone else.

I keep praying for the person I will be able to share the Good News with—someone who is ready to receive it but needs someone to talk to.

Lesson Learned #27

The young lady who was going to sell my Gifts back to me made me realize something that I suspected: many people are being offered or receiving multiple Gifts. This may explain some rejections—they already have one. It made me wonder which person I had given the most.

To somewhat compensate for this, I began visiting different metro stations and tried to change the time I visited a station by ten or fifteen minutes. It makes sense that many people leave work at the same time each day and arrive at the metro station at the same time, give or take a few minutes. But since there are so many people who enter each station between four and seven in the evening, I can work it out so I won't see the same people all the time.

Friday, August 16, 1991

A guy asked me what religion the book was. He had been reading it after I gave it to him. I answered his question and shared the *Four Spiritual Laws* with him. I asked if he wanted to pray. He said not now. I was excited that we had progressed so far even though he said no to praying to accept Jesus.

Monday, August 19, 1991

I gave a Gift to a young man from Afghanistan. He said he was a Christian. I went over the *Four Spiritual Laws* with him, and he prayed with me and accepted Jesus. *Praise the Lord! This was the first time someone prayed with me and accepted Jesus Christ as his Lord and Savior.* After praying, we discussed growing in Christ.

I spoke with an elderly lady. She was telling me about the bargains she finds. She goes to a non-denominational church at Ft. Myer. I went over the *Four Spiritual Laws* with her. When I asked her if she wanted to pray, she said she wanted to show it to her pastor.

Lesson Learned #28

It is becoming clearer and clearer to me that people waiting for a bus don't seem to mind talking. It's a great opportunity to share Jesus with them.

Tuesday, August 20, 1991

After handing out my Gifts, I gave one to a Spanish-speaking man from Peru. He understood the *Four Spiritual Laws* pretty well. I prayed with him, and he received Jesus.

Wednesday, August 21, 1991

On my way over to the metro station, I saw three friends from my workplace, standing out front of the building. One asked me if I was going over to pass out my Jehovah's Witness info. I said I was going over, but I wasn't handing out Jehovah's Witness info. I asked him if he would like one. He said, "Yes," and I gave him one. I need to look now for an opportunity to ask if he has had a chance to read it.

I thought it was interesting that he knew that I was passing something out at the metro train station. Made me wonder who he had heard it from and what they talked about.

After passing out Gifts, I sat with a young Spanish man and gave him a Gift. He didn't speak much English, so I gave him a Spanish *Four Spiritual Laws*. I went through it in English, and he read the Spanish. After we prayed and he asked Jesus into his heart, I went over to the Gannet Building for coffee. I gave a Gift to a man—a cook. I asked if he was a Christian, and I found out he sings in two choirs at his church.

Thursday, August 22, 1991

I shared the *Four Spiritual Laws* with a man who had trouble with English but insisted he understood. I prayed for him, and he agreed in prayer.

Lesson Learned #29

No fruit without roots. When I first started witnessing, I was nervous and worried about what people would think (of me), but I didn't give up. I persevered, and after a while, I began to produce fruits. As scripture says, "Blessed is the man who trusts in the Lord, whose trust is the Lord. He is like a tree planted by water, that sends out its roots by the stream, and does not fear when heat comes, for its leaves remain green, and is not anxious in the year of drought, for it does not cease to bear fruit" (Jeremiah 17:7–8).

In the beginning, I lacked confidence and was somewhat awkward in my presentation. I suspect people noticed this, but I trusted in the Lord, and once I established my roots, I began to produce fruit. As I grew more confident, people were more willing to listen and respond.

Friday, August 23, 1991

I shared with a Muslim woman. She let me go through the *Four Spiritual Laws* but didn't want to pray to accept Jesus.

I went to the Rockville Metro Train Station. One fellow became very hostile. He told me he was a Muslim, and religion was for the weak and that it wasn't scientific—it couldn't be proven. He muttered something about there not being a God. I asked him if he worshiped God in his Muslim faith. He said, "No," and that he was in it for social reasons. He finally left, and I finished handing out my *Four Spiritual Laws*.

Lesson Learned #4

Some people that you witness to will disagree, even argue with you. Be kind and understanding. Listen to what they are saying. You don't have to agree with them, but be kind and gentle. Scripture reminds us we are to:

- "Always be prepared to make a defense to any one who calls you to account for the hope that is in you, yet do it with gentleness and reverence" (1 Peter 3:15).
- "Let your speech always be gracious, seasoned with salt, so that you may know how you ought to answer every one" (Colossians 4:6).

Remember that your goal is not to win arguments but to win souls to Jesus. Even though you know you could win the argument, don't. If you win the argument, you may lose the soul that you are trying to save.

Tuesday, August 27, 1991

One man was really happy to get a Gift.

A woman put on a big, sincere smile and said thanks.

I shared the *Four Spiritual Laws* with a mother and daughter. They were Hispanic. I prayed with them, and they received Christ. I wasn't sure about approaching two women. They were both looking at the Gift I had given them. I talked with them and then shared the *Four Spiritual Laws*. I was really feeling blessed. Dwight came over, and I told him the two women had just received Jesus. They agreed that they had, and Dwight gave them some new Christian advice.

Thursday, August 29, 1991

I had a discussion with Dwight about his church and how he uses tracts. The conversation was very one-sided. I only got a few words in. It was quite all right with me. I want to learn from his experience.

I went to the Rockville Metro Train Station, and while I was waiting for my daughter to pick me up, I sat down next to a man reading a Scientology newspaper. I shared the *Four Spiritual Laws* with him. When I came to the prayer part, he said he was already a Christian and that he had just picked up the paper.

Tuesday, September 10, 1991

I shared the *Four Spiritual Laws* with a man and prayed with him to receive Jesus as Lord and Savior.

I gave a bunch of *Four Spiritual Laws* (Spanish version) to Dwight.

Friday, September 13, 1991

I shared the *Four Spiritual Laws* with a homeless man. He knows he needs to return to the Lord but hasn't yet. He was hungry so I bought him something from Hardy's.

I shared the *Four Spiritual Laws* with a woman who seemed very excited. She said she wasn't a Christian. She didn't want to pray.

In the evening, I handed out about thirty *Four Spiritual Laws* at Metro Center Train Station and about fifteen at Gallery Place Metro Train Station. I looked for people to whom I felt the Lord was leading me to give one. One pregnant woman, a Christian, was really excited about it because it was from the Bible.

I gave a Gift to a homeless woman who was panhandling and wanted money, and she stopped what she was doing to read it.

I gave a Gift to a man who was reading the Bible. He is a Pentecostal. He really memorized the Word and placed it in his heart. He was very encouraging.

I met a woman, also a Christian. She and her husband work in the southeast with youth.

At the end of the day, I was really encouraged and felt the presence of Jesus and his yoke upon me.

Wednesday, September 18, 1991

I shared the *Four Spiritual Laws* with a woman who prayed with me, accepting Jesus as her Lord and Savior. This happened while I was conversing with John. I excused myself and shared with her after she sat down.

There was a man who couldn't keep his hands off of a woman (both homeless). I approached them and offered him a Gift. He gave me a funny look and gave it to her. He didn't want anything to do with me.

Thursday, September 19, 1991

One of my last Gifts went to a Pentecostal. All he could talk about was his church. He didn't seem to understand the importance of Jesus. It was his church, speaking in tongues, and baptism in the Spirit that he wanted to talk about. I prayed for him. Since he was Spanish-speaking, I gave him a Spanish version of the *Four Spiritual Laws*. He used to be Catholic but became Pentecostal.

I gave a Gift to a man who said he used to be an atheist but wasn't anymore. I was glad to hear that.

Friday, September 20, 1991

I gave away twenty-four Gifts. A young man started to ask me questions before I had finished handing out my Gifts for the day. My reaction was to brush him off. I realized his questions really were more important than passing out my Gifts. I stopped to talk and shared the *Four Spiritual Laws* with him. He was in St. Elizabeth's and about to be released to a halfway house.

I find myself more willing to talk to people. This evening at Metro Center Train Station, I gave a Gift to a young man with earphones. He kind of rejected me. Then we talked. He is a college student and in a Bible study. He knows the Word quite well. He told me to smile more. He asked me to visit his Bible study. I said no. I should have said yes or at least considered it.

I shared with a Christian woman who was down in the dumps because of her work situation. We prayed for her situation. She was encouraged after our conversation and prayer.

I shared the *Four Spiritual Laws* with an elderly man, but he didn't want to pray.

Another man got impatient after law 2. He said he would read it on his own.

I thanked the Lord for such a great day.

Lesson Learned #30

Whenever people seem interested and want to talk, I should stop what I am doing, focus on them, and follow the lead of the Holy Spirit. This is what I want to do with all that the Lord brings to me. My problem is that sometimes I don't recognize it right away, and I stand a chance of the person wandering off.

Monday, September 23, 1991

I gave a Gift to a woman from work. She said, "So this is what you do with your spare time."

I shared the *Four Spiritual Laws* with an Indian man from South Africa. He prayed and accepted Jesus as his Lord and Savior. I was hesitant about sharing with him, but I decided to trust the Lord and not depend on my preconceived notions. I am sure that I will learn more about this in the future.

Thursday, September 26, 1991

I met an entomologist (insect specialist) on his way to Egypt and Israel. He volunteered using his vacation. At one time, he belonged to a fundamentalist community that traveled around. He is married. We discussed the woman at the well. He was very knowledgeable. He noticed my Gospel of John. I gave him one. He wants me to write him. He highly recommended a book, *The World Turned Upside-Down*. I looked it up on Amazon and found quite a few books with that title. I should have asked him for the author's name as well.

Thursday, October 10, 1991

I sat down with a young lady reading a Gospel of John. She is Catholic and had received Jesus as her Lord and Savior. She firmly knew it. She has a friend in Rockville. I invited her to the Children of Light prayer meeting. I really felt uplifted and encouraged.

Friday, October 11, 1991

I sat next to a man and shared the *Four Spiritual Laws* with him. He is a seventy-three-year-old Baptist who worked at an Episcopal church. He had already accepted Christ.

I started to share with two Hispanic women. I only got through the first law.

I shared with a young college-aged woman. We made it through the first two laws, and her bus came.

After work, I went to the Metro Center Train Station. One man asked me for few extra *Four Spiritual Laws* to pass out. He knew someone at Here's Life.

There was a group with a drum who were street dancing. They made lots of noise.

Lesson Learned #31

One disadvantage of evangelizing at a bus stop is that you may be in the middle of sharing with a person and the bus comes. If you are using the *Four Spiritual Laws*, then it is best to give it to the person and ask them to finish reading it. This might be a good opportunity to leave a phone number or an email in case they want to talk or have any questions. You could ask them to let you know what they think.

Tuesday, October 22, 1991

I shared the *Four Spiritual Laws* with a Spanish man. He read the prayer. About halfway through, he asked my religion. When I told him I was Catholic, he let me continue.

I shared the *Four Spiritual Laws* with a big young man. He was Muslim. He didn't want to pray.

Thursday, October 24, 1991

I prayed with two men. Both said they were Baptists. One said he was Catholic (this was the first time I had heard of a Baptist Catholic). I prayed with the other. He was a tall man and looked like a basketball player. He said he works with young kids.

Friday, October 25, 1991

I spoke with a man waiting for the bus. He didn't take a Gift. He quoted Jesus telling the lame man to take up his pallet and walk. He quoted it in Arabic (I think).

I gave out fifty *Four Spiritual Laws* at Metro Center Train Station on the way home. I had no new observations.

Monday, October 28, 1991

I gave a Gift to one of the janitors at my workplace who walked by the Rosslyn Metro Train Station.

Tuesday, October 29, 1991

A man took a Gift and immediately threw it right into the trash can. He missed, and I picked it up.

A Spanish woman with a two-year-old girl asked to borrow a dollar so she could ride the metro. I gave her a Spanish Gospel of John and a dollar.

Wednesday, October 30, 1991

I saw an executive from work on the skywalk, and I gave him a Gift. We had a brief discussion but of no substance. I told him that I hand them out at lunchtime.

A young lady with whom I had shared the *Four Spiritual Laws* the other day sat down and talked with me. She had prayed the *Four Spiritual Laws* prayer and knew Jesus was in her heart. She had some doubts. I encouraged her to read her Bible and to find a good church to attend.

Thursday, October 31, 1991

I met an energetic young Spanish man. He called me Pedro. I gave him a copy of the *Four Spiritual Laws* in Spanish. We were reading through it when his bus came.

Wednesday, November 6, 1991

I had a long discussion with a Buddhist. He was convinced his was the only way because it was logical. I brought up the problem with reincarnation, and he brought up the pope, infallibility, and the Trinity, none of which he agreed with. I was rushed and frustrated. I was preparing for a presentation I had to do at work, so I didn't do very well with my apologetics. I should have used the Sword of the Spirit, but I didn't.

I spoke with a Korean lady selling ties. She was a Christian. I gave her another Gift. She said we would talk some more later. I enjoyed talking with her.

Lesson Learned #32

Apologetics contains a large number of issues, but each of them is important. Some important rules for being an apologist are:

- Study, study, and study issues in your spare time.
- Be accepting of the other person but not necessarily his or her point of view.
- If you don't know the answer to a question, say you don't know and that you will research it and get back to the person (try for an appointment).
- If you are going to use a scripture, know the book, chapter, and verse. Otherwise, don't use it.
- Be polite. You don't just want to win the battle and lose the war.

Thursday, November 7, 1991

At the Rockville Metro Train Station, one young lady returned her *Four Spiritual Laws* and said she didn't need it. She said she didn't believe in God and then ran off.

Friday, November 8, 1991

I was at Shady Grove. Boy was it ever cold. Two men and a woman were very encouraging. When they saw me, they said, "Praise the Lord!" The woman told me she had to start carrying her Bible. She had been a backslider but has come back to the Lord.

Tuesday, November 12, 1991

I met an elderly lady who told me she has twenty-six grandchildren—what a ministry! She reminded me of my grandmother. She has been a Christian for over twenty-five years and said the Lord has really blessed her.

Thursday, November 14, 1991

I smiled more today, and it went faster. One person took two Gifts and asked for another one. I also gave him a Redskins tract.

I gave John a Redskins tract. The Redskins are the Washington DC football team.

Lesson Learned #33

It is really important to smile. People seem to be more receptive and open when you do. I guess when you look too serious, people must suspect you are up to no good.

Friday, November 15, 1991

I was at the Shady Grove Metro Train Station when I met a man who works for Amtrak. He sometimes attends St. Mary's Church. We discussed the Gospel of John, and he gave me a dollar donation. I took it because I didn't want to hurt his feelings.

I met a woman from the Church of the Redeemer. She encouraged me.

The flower vendor gave me his last bunch of flowers and

said it was for the good work I was doing. I gave them to my wife.

Wednesday, November 20, 1991

I gave out some Redskins tracts at the Rosslyn Metro Train Station after work. While I think this is a really cool tract, many people rejected it. At first, I thought they didn't want anything that was religious, but after thinking it out, I decided it may have been just because they weren't Redskins fans. Some great plans just backfire.

Friday, November 22, 1991

It was slow moving. I think because the weather was so bad and people just wanted to get home as soon as possible.

I gave the *Four Spiritual Laws* in Korean to the lady at the sandwich shop, the tie vendor, and the Korean man at the office supply store.

On the way home, I went to Shady Grove Metro Train Station and gave out a hundred *Four Spiritual Laws* and one pack of Redskins' tracts (fifty?).

I saw the lady from the Church of the Redeemer again.

The flower vendors gave me flowers again. I gave them both a Redskins tract.

I met a young Christian man who is very committed to Christ. He told me that he has the gift of prophesy and has seen visions. He helped me pass out tracts.

Monday, November 25, 1991

I shared *Four Spiritual Laws* with a woman, and while we were sharing, a man interrupted and gave her a tract. I spoke with him later. He was a new Baptist. I shared my testimony and encouraged him to resist sin and temptation.

He had lots of questions, which I answered. He had a *Plain Truth* magazine, which I told him to ask his pastor about. I gave him a Gift.

Tuesday, December 3, 1991

I met a man who was saved through the Gospel of John five or six years ago. We talked for a while, and he said it was the same John but a different him (the Gospel of John was the same, but he had become a new creation in Christ).

While I was handing out Gifts, a man stood by reading his copy. He was a pizza man (made sauce and dough) from New York and a Christian. He had been on an interview (five hundred people for fifty jobs). It was with UPS and was a temporary position for only ten days during the Christmas season. He was sure the end times are here, and Jesus will come soon.

Thursday, December 5, 1991

I had a hostile confrontation today. The man could hardly see. He took a Gift and put it up close to his face. The way he was talking, I thought there might be something wrong with him. When he found out I was a born-again Christian, he got mad because he was a Jew and the Christians were trying to convert all his people to Christianity. He threw the Gift back at me. He then threatened violence if I didn't get out of his face. He was using bad language and was very angry.

I told him he was entitled to his opinion, and I continued to hand out my Gifts. He kind of hung around for a few minutes and then disappeared. I wasn't afraid, nor did I want to strike back. I was able to look at him with compassion. I felt bad he believed a lie and was so resistant to the truth. I prayed after that God would lift the scales from his eyes.

I stopped at Wheaton Metro Train Station on my way home and passed out fifty *Four Spiritual Laws*.

Lesson Learned #34

When facing someone who is angry or violent, keep the following tips in mind.

- Pray for help.
- Don't strike back.
- Avoid the person if possible.
- Move away from him or her.

Friday, December 6, 1991

Today, the peanut man and a Spanish man both wanted to talk. I took more time handing out Gifts than usual. I didn't mind. I enjoyed the conversation. I wanted to be sensitive to the Spirit. I have been asking for an opportunity to look upon people with the same compassion Jesus has when he looks upon me.

One lady came back three times. She offered a dollar, but I refused. She gave one Gift away and wanted one for her son.

In the evening, I stopped at Metro Center Train Station and handed out Redskins tracts. I wore my Redskins hat.

I ministered to one person who used to go to church. I encouraged him to go back. I gave him a Gift.

A couple of men were really impressed with the Redskins tract. One said, "I really like this." The other smiled when he saw people taking it because of the Skins picture on it.

Friday, December 13, 1991

I was blessed by a woman with a "Jesus Is the Reason for the Season" pin.

Another man wanted to give me a donation. I said it wasn't necessary.

A few people wished me a Merry Christmas. They must have the Christmas spirit.

At the Rockville Metro Train Station in the evening, I gave a man a Redskins tract, and he asked me why the Skins were kneeling. (I don't think he read the tract.) When I told him they believed in Jesus, he got mad and said they didn't. Later he came back and said he was sorry.

Friday, December 20, 1991

I gave away Gifts in the evening at Fort Totten Metro Train Station. Mostly people were very receptive. One man came back and said it was just what he needed. He was in a Bible study studying the Gospel of John.

A woman asked me how long I had been a Christian. I told her since April 15, 1974. We both praised God and agreed he was good.

Tuesday, December 24, 1991

I gave away Gifts at Metro Center Train Station. I wished each person a Merry Christmas. Most of them were receptive.

One lady encouraged me. She was a missionary. Many came and asked me for one of what I was handing out.

Friday, December 31, 1991

Sometimes I try to guess whether a person will accept my gift. I shouldn't do this because it may cause me to withhold a Gift from someone who really needs one.

Lesson Learned #35

I must be very careful not to judge. I can usually tell whether a person will accept a tract, but I want to be sure, so I offer one to everyone regardless. Sometimes I am surprised when someone I thought wouldn't be interested takes one.

CHAPTER 10

Year Two

Paul planted, Apollos watered, but God gave the
growth. So neither he who plants nor he who
waters is anything, but only God who gives the
growth.

—1 Corinthians 3:6–7

Friday, January 3, 1992

Two Christian men thanked me and shook my hand. One
was a minister who had a church in DC. We shared the
importance of getting the Word out and the futility of those
who trust in themselves and their money.

I sat down with an elderly Spanish man. I had already
given him a Gift. He had locked himself out of his car. The
key was in the car, and he was waiting for someone to come
to help him open it. I started to share the *Four Spiritual Laws*
with him. He told me he had been a Christian for the last ten

years. After law 1, he effectively changed the conversation. Then remembering he was Spanish, I told him I was learning the language and asked him to help me with reading the Spanish version of the *Four Spiritual Laws*. This worked. We discussed the importance of reaching Spanish people. He was a Baptist. He left to call someone.

Tuesday, January 14, 1992

After work, I went to Fort Totten Metro Train Station. One man read the whole *Four Spiritual Laws* booklet, it seemed. He was waiting for someone. I should have approached him to see if he had any questions.

Friday, January 17, 1992

One woman said flat-out nastily, "No! I don't want one," when I offered her a Gift on the bench.

Another woman told me she couldn't read. I told her there were programs to help her to learn how. She said she was in one at the library. I shared the *Four Spiritual Laws* with her, but she turned away and didn't really want to hear. She got up and left as soon as she saw her bus coming down the street.

That evening, I stopped at Metro Center Train Station and gave away about a hundred miscellaneous tracts that I had accumulated. One man was very drunk and tried to hug and kiss me. He asked me if I died, if I would go to heaven and if anything could hurt me. He said he had been saved. He believed that "once saved, always saved," even if drunk.

Another man, a Muslim, I think, gave me a hard time. I gave him a *Four Spiritual Laws*. He wanted to know what *spiritual* meant. When I told him the Spirit of God, he told me I confused him by using the same word. We discussed the Trinity, and he claimed it was made up by Christians and that Jesus wasn't the Messiah. He wanted to argue. Finally, his bus came. I said, "God bless you."

Tuesday, January 21, 1992

This evening, I gave away Redskins tracts at Grosvenor Metro Train Station. I specifically tried to get people to take one based on the Redskins picture. You could tell those who looked at the picture and then decided to take one.

One young lady asked what it was, and I told her it was about the Redskins. She said she didn't care about them. That kind of backfired. I thought if I mentioned the Redskins, she would naturally want one. But in this case, since she didn't like the Redskins, she rejected the tract. I vowed, no more trickery. She asked if I was mad at her because she didn't take one. I told her I wasn't.

Wednesday, January 22, 1992

One woman identified herself as a Christian and asked for more tracts. I gave her a half a dozen.

One woman made a lot of noise to her friend and tossed her Gift into the trash.

Thursday, January 23, 1992

In the evening, I went to the Rockville Metro Train Station and gave away Redskins tracts. Many seemed glad to receive them. There were only a few rejections. One man came back and took one after saying he already had one. He said he had better take one since he hadn't been truthful.

Monday, February 3, 1992

I have decided to spend more time giving out Gifts. I will be more laid-back—less forceful. It will take longer but may provide more opportunity for individual ministry.

I shared the *Four Spiritual Laws* with a woman who was

a Christian. She wanted the Gift and *Four Spiritual Laws* to take to her Bible study at Carroll House in Virginia.

Wednesday, February 5, 1992

One man came back and asked which church I was with. I told him the Catholic church—St. Mary's in Rockville. He thought I had come all the way down to distribute tracts. He said I was building up treasures in heaven—each tract was a coin in my heavenly bank account.

Thursday, February 6, 1992

Today, I met one man who wondered what I was giving out. When I held it up for him to look at, he said no but came back for one. I sensed that God was pleased with him because he came back. However, only God knows a person's motives.

Tuesday, February 11, 1992

I met a man who had a TV repair business. We talked a lot. He knew the Lord's telephone number 1-800-Jer 33:3—"Call to me and I will answer you, and will tell you great and hidden things that you have not known" (Jeremiah 33:3). He had a very special gift and could make an acronym out of anything.

Wednesday, February 12, 1992

I had lunch with my friend Gerry today. He picked me up at the Rosslyn Metro Train Station and saw me handing out the Gifts. I asked if he wanted one. He said no but changed his mind. He said he would look through it. I told him about my ministry. I gave him a *Four Spiritual Laws*. He said I was the first evangelist he knew. I shared about my conversion and how I became a Catholic. He said he never asked me about my conversion in Rochester (he was my boss at the time) because some people don't talk about religion. He said he did want to know. I agreed to share my testimony the next time we met for lunch.

Thursday, February 13, 1992

One young lady asked for another Gift for her friend.

A woman at Hardy's asked for change. I asked her what for, and she said something to eat. I bought her a cheeseburger and a Coke.

Friday, February 14, 1992, Valentine's Day

I met a nice young Christian man. He worked for another Christian who had a business installing accounting software. He distributed thousands of tracts in college.

Thursday, February 20, 1992

I gave away eighteen Gifts. I saw Michael (the deacon). He asked for a copy of the Gospel of John. He said he was hoping to see me today. He wanted to give it to a friend. It made me feel good that he was looking for me and hoping I would be there.

Friday, February 21, 1992

I felt lifted up and encouraged. I couldn't wait to hand out *Four Spiritual Laws* at Metro Center Train Station.

One woman blessed me and said those who reject will be sorry someday.

Another lady asked for some *Four Spiritual Laws* tracts

to hand out at her apartment. I gave her the 800 number to order some. I should have given her a "how-to" booklet.

One man recognized me. He read through the *Four Spiritual Laws* and then gave it back to me. He was a small man. I think he was homeless. He said he never took one from me. I didn't argue. I was really uplifted.

Wednesday, February 26, 1992

A man changed his mind and said, "Yes, I'll take one." He asked whom I was with. I told him I was from St Mary's. He said that was where F. Scott Fitzgerald was from. He asked why the book of John. I told him it was clear and easy to read and understand.

Friday, March 6, 1992

Dwight Moody was there today. While we were talking, a woman who seemed homeless came up to us. Dwight tried to share the *Four Spiritual Laws* with her. She let him get past the first page. He asked if she was a Christian. She said yes that she was an Episcopalian. We both tried to get her to tell us she had received Jesus as her Lord and Savior, but she never did. She kept changing the subject. She knew scripture well enough to quote it but wouldn't profess Jesus as her Lord. She kept talking about how she and been cut open in the head by a machine, but I couldn't see a scar.

I spoke with the young man who hangs out with the T-shirt vendor. He works for the Arlington Hospital as a maintenance man. He is an agnostic—not sure if there is a god. He has a spider tattoo on his neck. He said he is a Cactus (mother a Catholic and father a Baptist).

On the way home, I stopped at Metro Center Train Station and gave out 150 *Four Spiritual Laws*.

Tuesday, March 10, 1992

I was kind of down today, but the Lord lifted me up. One man thanked me. He said I had good books. He spoke Spanish, so I asked him if he would like a Spanish version. He said yes and thanked me.

A young man told me he believed in God but not necessarily the Christian God. He didn't believe in hell. His religious beliefs were private. He listened to the *Four Spiritual Laws* but didn't want to pray.

Wednesday, March 11, 1992

I met a Spanish Woman and gave her a copy of "Juan" and a Spanish version of the *Four Spiritual Laws*. She shared a problem with me after asking if I was Catholic. She went to St. Agnes. Her nephew was in Peru and had children. When he went to have them baptized, he was told he would have to go through a preparation class. There also was some problem about him being married outside of the church. Her concern (she lost sleep over it the night before) was what would happen to the children if they died before being baptized.

I tried to comfort her. I told her God would take care of them. I suggested she pray to God for them and see her priest.

Friday, March 13, 1992

A man was loading his truck and said he would get one later. After I was done, I went inside the metro station, and he followed me in. He asked me for another copy for his wife. He read the King James Version.

That evening, I went to the Rockville Metro Train Station and gave out a hundred *Four Spiritual Laws*. Nothing unusual happened, and there were no new observations.

Monday, March 16, 1992

I gave away St. Patrick's Day tracts. Many people took the tract because it said "St. Patrick" on it. It was very cold.

In the evening, I went to Tenleytown Metro Train Station and gave out fifty St. Patrick tracts on each side of Wisconsin Avenue. People seemed interested in getting the tract.

Tuesday, March 17, 1992 (St. Patrick's Day)

In the morning, I gave away St. Patrick tracts at the Rosslyn Station. People were very receptive. About 75 percent actually smiled at me when they saw what it was.

I gave one to a good friend who worked in personnel (and is quite Irish). She asked why I was handing out tracts. I explained it to her.

I gave one to a lady in the Latin American Department.

I gave one to a lady (I think she is my friend Lois's friend). She teaches English as a second language. She asked for a few more to share with her class. What a great way to learn English!

At lunchtime, I gave out St. Patrick tracts. All seemed eager to receive. I gave about half of them to a busload of kids who went into the metro station.

Thursday, March 19, 1992

I gave a Korean vendor a *Four Spiritual Laws*. She actually asked if I was going to give it to her while I was thinking how I would do it.

Monday, March 23, 1992

I gave a Gift to Lois's friend who was passing by and had a chat with her. She then went up to the health store. She gave her Gift to a man there and came back for another. She left and then came back and said how sad it was to see all those people who were passing by and rejecting the free Gift. Someday, they will be sorry.

Tuesday, March 24, 1992

I gave a Gift to a volunteer at work. She thought it was nice what I was doing. She passed by again and asked what my congregation was. I told her it was St. Mary's in Rockville.

Thursday, March 26, 1992

Slow today. Many rejections. One young lady smiled a big smile and then an army officer right after her said he had one and then squeezed my arm. This encouraged me.

One man violently threw the Gift into the trash. I retrieved it and gave it to someone else.

Friday, March 27, 1992

I was encouraged by one lady who worships at Beth Messiah. She said they may reject because they don't know what it is. She almost did that until she saw what it was. She was blessed, and so was I.

Wednesday, April 1, 1992

I met a man from the Bible Way Church in Washington DC. He had thick glasses and didn't realize I was giving him a Gospel of John. He saw the bread on the cover and thought it was cake and that it might be a recipe book. He made a phone call and came back. We praised the Lord together. I tried to help him get his bus.

Friday, April 3, 1992

Today, four ladies from work passed by. They each took a Gift. They didn't realize what it was until they got the book.

Lesson Learned #36

People don't always know what I am offering and may reject my offer just because they don't want to be bothered and not necessarily because they are not interested.

Monday, April 6, 1992

It was a nice spring day. I prayed with a woman who received the Lord after going over the *Four Spiritual Laws*. She was having trouble with her children because of the influences of this world on them. I prayed with her.

Thursday, April 9, 1992

I met a woman with lots of problems. She had just split from her boyfriend and was trying to "find herself" and make something of herself. She left her boyfriend because he acted like a little kid. He was forty-six or so and big—six foot something.

When I gave her a Gift, she said she was Catholic and wasn't going to convert. She was surprised when I told her I was Catholic. She opened up. I told her I would pray for her.

Tuesday, April 14, 1992

I gave a Gift to a metro driver. He was reading it over and over. I asked him if he was familiar with the Bible. He was disturbed that John 20:17 in the KJV said Jesus said he ascended to His Father, whereas other translations said He would ascend. The man was very upset that someone was lying and asked why there were new versions. He must have been a "King James Only" person. I said the more contemporary version is better understood by people of today and more consistent with the language usage of today. I need to study that passage in case I see him again.

Another woman came back and gave me a pamphlet from the Church of God.

I had specifically asked God for some excitement, and I guess the metro driver was it.

Friday, April 17, 1992

I distributed a whole shipment at Metro Center (408). This was for my birthday.

Today was Good Friday.

One workman came up to me and chatted. He was a Baptist. He gave me encouragement. A few others did also. I was there for about two hours. Two people asked for two copies. A couple passed by and came back.

One man with his head partially shaved kept walking in and out of the metro. He was yelling and cursing. He kept coming out, and a number of times, I tried to offer him a Gift and he refused.

Sunday, April 19, 1992

It's my birthday! Hallelujah! Jesus Christ is risen indeed! What a joy and cause to celebrate your birthday when it happens on the same day as Easter. Praise the Lord!

Thursday, April 23, 1992

I shared with a young man. He prayed with me to receive Jesus. He said he never got over here, but for some reason, he did today. It sounds like a divine appointment to me.

After he left, two men sat on my bench. I waited and gave them a Gift and *Four Spiritual Laws*. One was a Christian and the other Muslim. I asked God for guidance. I saw this as a chance to preach to a group. I wasn't aggressive enough. The Christian said he would read it at home. I need to be a bit more assertive.

I gave a copy of "Juan" to a Spanish woman. She didn't seem very comfortable. She came back later and was reading the Spanish *Four Spiritual Laws*. I should have tried my Spanish on her. Maybe I should develop a dialogue using Spanish.

Lesson Learned #37

Sharing the gospel with a group creates a different dynamic than sharing with one person. People are less open when others are around. They don't know what others think and accordingly may be less open to accepting what they are hearing.

Wednesday, April 29, 1992

I prayed with two men today. First, there was a young Spanish man waiting for his brother. I gave him a copy of "Juan" and *Four Spiritual Laws* for his brother. I explained the *Four Spiritual Laws* in English while he followed along with me in Spanish. He prayed the prayer to receive Jesus as Lord and Savior. He didn't belong to a church, so I encouraged him to find and join one.

The other man was a retired man who wasn't sure he was a Christian. He said he was a Methodist but didn't attend church regularly. We went over the *Four Spiritual Laws*. He was mumbling, so I couldn't be sure if he read the prayer. I asked him, and he said he did. He was a carpenter but didn't do much with his trade.

Thursday, April 30, 1992

I distributed Gifts at Rockville Metro Train Station.

I met a man who was eighty-two and a Christian. He belonged to the Presbyterian Church. He was very active as an elder. His wife played the organ and led the choir for twenty-five years. He said she was the best Christian ever and felt she went straight to heaven. When she died, the nurse called him and said she had never seen such a glow when someone died. He was retired US Air Force and always prayed that he wouldn't be a cripple. The problem today is people don't pray. He loved John because Jesus loved John. It's the book of love. He talked to the other seniors to encourage them. He said all that matters is that you have Jesus in your heart and a spring in your step. It was a very wonderful, uplifting conversation.

I spoke with the T-shirt vendor for quite a while. He was asking which book I preached. He seemed to be searching. He had a copy of "the Book," which I think was a Living Bible. I suggested he begin with John. We got into a discussion about his mother, who died of Alzheimer's. He shared some of his struggles and hardships. For eight years, his father was a Baptist and his mother a Catholic. After his father left, he became Catholic and went to Catholic school. He seemed to have struggles with organized religion, but he was searching.

Wednesday, May 6, 1992

I bought a picture of Jesus in the garden knocking on the door from the T-shirt vendor. It is by William Holden Hunt, and it is called "The Light of the World." The flower vendor was there at the same time. I explained why there was no doorknob on the door. They were amazed when I told them. They had never noticed it before. Even the flower vendor said, "He must be knocking for me." It was kind of a plea worth regarding.

Monday, May 11, 1992

I shared a *Four Spiritual Laws* with a young man. He prayed the prayer with me to accept Jesus as his Lord and Savior. He seemed somewhat preoccupied. He didn't talk much.

Wednesday, May 13, 1992

I gave a Gift to a woman who liked to talk. She was an Episcopalian. She was also a Unitarian. She told me all about it when I asked her. I recommended that she return to the church, which she said she doesn't attend much, and that she go back to singing in the choir. She told me she was sixty and had lost her voice but sounded nice to me when she sang a few lines.

I spoke with an elderly man with quite a few teeth missing. He didn't attend church, but you could tell he had had a Godly upbringing.

I gave a copy of "Juan" to a Spanish man, and we went through the *Four Spiritual Laws*. He didn't want to pray with me but said he would pray by himself. We didn't communicate very well.

Thursday, May 14, 1992

I gave out Gifts at Wheaton Metro Train Station, and there were many rejections. I prayed for a renewed vision and passion for those who were lost. I wanted to be more committed and single focused and to stop wasting my time on those things that distracted me from this goal.

I met a Spanish lady who had been here three years. She wanted to speak better English. I shared my desire to speak better Spanish. I gave her a copy of "Juan" and a *Four Spiritual Laws*.

I met an elderly lady from a Church of God. She said she was an evangelist. We talked of those who rejected Jesus. She said to shake the dust off our shoes. I quoted, "He who hears you hears me, and he who rejects you rejects me, and he who rejects me rejects him who sent me" (Luke 10:16–17).

I shared a Gift and *Four Spiritual Laws* with a man in his late twenties dressed in shorts with a bib and teenager clothes. He had had nothing to do with Christians or church or the Bible since he was a little child. He held the *Four Spiritual Laws*, and we went through them. When we reached the prayer, he said, "No," and chuckled, but he kept on reading.

I gave a Gift and a *Four Spiritual Laws* to a Muslim lady. She was very nice and talkative. I asked her how they (Muslims) handled sin and shared with her what Jesus did for all of us. They believe at judgment God weighs good and bad and rewards accordingly.

As I was waiting for the bus, I started to share with a man. His bus came. He was Catholic and went to St. Catherine's. He seemed interested.

I started to share with a woman who sat down next to me. She lived in the Aspen Hill area. She was Catholic but hadn't found a church yet. I told her about St. Patrick's and St. Mary's. Her daughter came while I was sharing the *Four Spiritual Laws* with her. The lady seemed interested, but her daughter was rude. She kept interrupting me. At law 2, the daughter said she wanted quality time with her mother. I stopped sharing. The woman thanked me before leaving.

Friday, May 15, 1992

I shared a Gift with an Arab lady who was a security guard at National Airport. Before sharing, I asked about her job. Because I showed the interest, she was more receptive to the *Four Spiritual Laws*. After reading, she asked if I was going to pray for her. When I asked for her name, she said she wanted me to see her Arabic Bible that she had in her purse, which she read every day but was glad to get the Gift so she could practice her English.

Lesson Learned #38

I find that when I show I am sincerely interested in the people I meet, they are more receptive when I share the Gift or *Four Spiritual Laws* with them. It only takes a second or two to observe a person and find something unique about him or her.

Monday, May 18, 1992

I had a nice chat with the elderly man with missing teeth. He is a real saint—a man of faith. We shared experiences—my witnessing, his dream where he woke up to a voice calling him. We had a good lengthy exchange, especially regarding faith.

I gave another elderly man a Gift and a *Four Spiritual Laws* and went through the *Four Spiritual Laws* with him. He prayed and received Jesus as his Lord and Savior. He had trouble seeing. He shared an experience where he was in great pain and all of a sudden the pain was lifted. He said he goes to church when he can, but it isn't as often as he would like. He takes his family with him. I should have offered to pray with him.

Tuesday, May 19, 1992

I gave a Gift and *Four Spiritual Laws* to a Georgetown student. She said she was a student and had a course in theology. She gave me back both but was willing to talk. She is a linguistics major. She is from Texas and spoke two languages as she grew up.

I shared and gave a Gift and *Four Spiritual Laws* to a young man. He said he is a photographer. He spoke softly. I was able to hear him pray and receive Jesus.

Friday, May 22, 1992

I shared with a fellow who was up from Newport News, Virginia, and looking for a job. He prayed with me and received Jesus as his Lord and Savior.

Wednesday, June 3, 1992

Today, I talked with an elderly lady (I had spoken with her before) from the House of Prayer church in DC. The church claims three million members in sixty churches throughout the United States.

Most of my time was spent with a young man who was a senior at Radcliffe College in Virginia. He was really worried about his girlfriend, who might be pregnant. They had a distance problem, and her folks didn't want them to be together. He was concerned because he hadn't heard from her. I tried to console him and just listen. We went through the *Four Spiritual Laws*, but he didn't want to pray to receive the Lord. He attended St. John's Episcopal Church in Olney.

I prayed today, asking for guidance. I feel the Lord is telling me to try to spend more time with those to whom the Lord leads me. It also occurred to me that there was time for passing out Gifts at metro train stations in the evening.

Friday, June 5, 1992

I met a man who transferred here from California. I gave him a Gift. He said his wife would like it. He was a Catholic. In California, they went to a nondenominational church. They were looking for a church here. I told him about the Church of the Redeemer.

I met a young man and gave him a Gift. He was active in soccer. He was friendly but not too open. He attends church at St. Mary's in Rockville.

Tuesday, June 9, 1992

I handed out a couple of Gifts. I met a lady who teaches English as a second language. I had spoken with her before. She shared how many hurting people she had seen. I wasn't sure what to do.

Wednesday, June 10, 1992

I prayed with John to receive Jesus.

I prayed with a man to receive Jesus. He was out of a job, living with his mother. He was a Catholic attending Nativity Church, but he needed to get his life back together first. God really surprised and blessed me richly today.

Thursday, June 11, 1992

I met a woman and gave her a *Four Spiritual Laws* and a Gift. She prayed the prayer to receive Jesus as her Lord and Savior. She was all alone with a twelve-year-old daughter and had experienced a lot of sickness.

I shared a Gift and a *Four Spiritual Laws* with a man who didn't want to pray the prayer to receive Jesus as his Lord and Savior. He was a Pentecostal at the age of seventeen. He left the church and wanted to "experience life." This was the first time I was faced with a backslider. Unfortunately, I didn't figure that out until after he had left. Lord, help me to learn to identify those who have strayed and encourage them to return to you.

Friday, June 12, 1992

I started to minister to a man who looked homeless. When I got into the *Four Spiritual Laws*, his bus arrived.

I shared the *Four Spiritual Laws* with a Catholic woman. She wanted to know about those who have never heard of Jesus. I shared Romans 1 with her. Her bus came before I could get to the *Four Spiritual Laws*.

I talked to the wild man. I tried to give him a Gift. He was incoherent. He didn't want the Gift I offered him.

I met another lady. I was really reluctant to share with her because she looked so hard. I was glad I did.

I gave out a hundred Gifts at the Wheaton Metro Train Station. It was fun to do after so long. It took about twenty minutes.

Some people you approach: the homeless, the down and out, and so on, may not look very appealing or attractive. I try to overlook how a person looks and appeal to the heart.

Lesson Learned #39

I must not look on the outward person but realize the inward person is the real one and the one seeking God. Just like scripture says in 1 Samuel 16:7, "But the Lord said to Samuel, 'Do not look on his appearance or on the height of his stature, because I have rejected him; for the Lord sees not as man sees; man looks on the outward appearance, but the Lord looks on the heart.'"

Monday June 15, 1992

I met a man who said he doesn't read the Bible (when I offered him a Gift). When I asked him why, he told me only about 50 percent of it was true. Each time I asked if he believed something, he said, "I don't believe it. I don't know it. I don't deny it." He felt he was covered with this statement. He was eighty plus. His wife was forty-four. He found God through Alcoholics Anonymous. He believed in the twelve steps because he did them. The only thing he believed was what he experienced and revelation from God. He had had a few revelations. He kept quoting Jesus, "The truth will make you free" (John 8:32). He was heavy into numerology. He used it because "numbers don't lie." He believed in the reincarnation of a spirit. He believed there were two Eves and one Adam, based on the creation of two females and one male. He knew when the world was going to end. He didn't believe in the virgin birth. He was quite an interesting man with many very strong opinions. I just listened to him.

I also met a young man who accepted Jesus through the *Four Spiritual Laws* and the prayer that he prayed. He was a friend of another Spanish man I prayed with to receive Jesus.

Tuesday, June 16, 1992

I offered a Gift to a Spanish woman from Bolivia. She was a Catholic and attended a Spanish Mass each Sunday afternoon. I gave her a copy of "Juan" and went through the *Four Spiritual Laws* with her. She spoke excellent English, so I quoted while she read. Then she prayed. We talked for a while.

Wednesday, June 17, 1992

I spoke with the homeless-looking man I had met last Friday. He was from Libya. He had two sons there who were in their thirties. He worked in a restaurant in DC. We talked for a while. He said he had read some of the Gospel of John that I had given him.

I shared with a tall man. He seemed kind of high on something. He was very interested and had questions. I started to share the *Four Spiritual Laws* with him, but he had to go. I gave him the *Four Spiritual Laws* booklet.

Friday, June 19, 1992

I shared the *Four Spiritual Laws* with a man who spoke little English. I wasn't going to go through the booklet but decided to anyway. He prayed and accepted the Lord. Even though I didn't want to put forth the effort, I was glad I did. Lord, never let me be lax again.

As I was getting ready to leave, I saw one of Lois's friends. I gave her a Gift. I was going to give her a *Four Spiritual Laws* booklet but decided to wait until I had an opportunity to share it with her.

I gave out sixty-six Gifts at Farragut North and Farragut West Metro Train Stations. I had lots of rejections from all groups. Many praised the Lord. I met one man from Christ Church.

Lesson Learned #40

When the Spirit uses you to share the Good News with someone, you should do just that regardless of your mood or how you feel. You will be pleasantly surprised with the fruit of your sharing. You just don't know what the person may be thinking, and you don't know how God may be working in his or her life. Your feelings or mood may be a result of an attack by the evil one who, of course, doesn't want you to succeed.

Monday, June 22, 1992

I shared the *Four Spiritual Laws* in Spanish with a very friendly young man. He was from El Salvador and had been here for about a year. We continued to talk after he accepted Jesus as his Lord and Savior. He told me he wanted to improve his English, and he understood I wanted to improve my Spanish.

I shared the *Four Spiritual Laws* with a man who prayed and received Jesus. He was out of work. I waited for his brother who shines shoes in the building next to the metro. Both men were very anxious and eager to receive Jesus.

Lesson Learned #41

Take the time to talk with people after praying with them for salvation. Try to find out more about them and what their needs are. Pray with them for their needs.

Wednesday, June 24, 1992

I gave a Gift to a Spanish man who didn't know English. I seemed really picky today. There were opportunities, but I didn't take them. Was it me or the Spirit?

Just before I left, I forced myself to share the *Four Spiritual Laws* with a tall, thin young man. He didn't say the prayer because he already had received the Lord. He prayed each morning. He didn't go to church much. He sometimes attended a church in Maryland and lived in Virginia. He had an ex-girlfriend who called him frequently. She invited him to church. He really appreciated my taking the time to talk with him.

Friday, June 26, 1992

I shared a *Four Spiritual Laws* with a man who was just taking a breather (not waiting for a bus). He was a Christian or trying to become one. We went through the *Four Spiritual Laws*, but he didn't pray to receive Jesus as his Lord and Savior.

I prayed with a man. He received Jesus.

I gave a Gift to the T-shirt vender.

I gave a Gift to a young man from Ethiopia. He professed to be a Christian. His bus came before we finished.

Monday, June 29, 1992

I met a man who is a Christian and loves Jesus. I went through the *Four Spiritual Laws* with him. I stressed getting into a church. He apparently hadn't been attending for the last four years.

As I was leaving, I offered a Gift to an elderly, well-dressed man. He immediately said, "No."

Tuesday, June 30, 1992

I spoke with the sunglasses vendor. He used to be a truck driver. He lost his license after two DWIs.

I spoke with a man who had been in Alcoholics Anonymous for a long time (twenty years) and had MS. They said he would never walk, but he was walking. He attributed this to the Lord. He knew the Serenity Prayer.

Tuesday, July 7, 1992

I prayed with a man who received Jesus as his Lord and Savior. He was very friendly. He reminded me of one of my nephews.

I had a long discussion with a Mormon who had just returned from his two-year mission trip. He had a great deal of trouble understanding God's grace. His sister was brutally killed—stabbed over a hundred times by her husband. He couldn't understand how God could forgive that man. Before he shared this with me, I shared how I came to the Lord. He used to be a Catholic. I went through the *Four Spiritual Laws* with him, but he didn't want to pray. This was a very interesting discussion. He was really hurting because of what had happened to his sister.

Monday, July 20, 1992

Today, I spent most of my time visiting with all the regulars and getting caught up with the latest news. I talked with the tie vendor. We became good friends. I gave her a Chinese Bible from the American Bible Society.

Tuesday, July 28, 1992

I gave away Gifts at Metro Center. It was a beautiful day. Lots of people out. I shared the *Four Spiritual Laws* with two men. One of them asked me to pray for him.

I went to share with a young lady. She said she didn't speak English. She was Russian. We chatted for a while (as best we could).

I gave away a hundred Gifts at Metro Center. Many were thankful.

I went with one man and bought him a meal at the Waffle House. He said I was a good man. Thank you, Jesus. I did it for you.

Thursday, July 30, 1992

I shared the *Four Spiritual Laws* with a woman who prayed with me and received Jesus as her Lord and Savior. She was looking for a job. We prayed concerning a job for her.

Friday, July 31, 1992

I gave away Gifts at the Rhode Island Metro Train Station.

I told a man about Jesus using the *Four Spiritual Laws*. He was a really big guy. He was very thankful for me taking the time but didn't want to pray.

I spoke with a man who didn't speak much English. I went through the Spanish version of the *Four Spiritual Laws*. He read the prayer accepting Jesus as his Lord and Savior.

I gave out a hundred Gifts. People were very receptive, and many thanked me. It was in the midst of a storm.

Monday, August 3, 1992

I shared Jesus with a young Catholic man. He attended St. James in Virginia. We went through the *Four Spiritual Laws*, but he didn't want to pray.

I shared the *Four Spiritual Laws* with a woman who was in the army. She prayed with me. We discussed the condition of this country and what the church should be doing.

Tuesday, August 4, 1992

I met an Egyptian who knew Jesus but hadn't been to church for years. He couldn't hold a job. He suffered from depression. I encouraged him to get back into a church.

I met a Seventh Day Adventist from Bread of Life Church in DC. He knew the scripture well. After a while, I realized he had a very legalistic argumentation style like other Adventists I know.

I gave out about fifty *Four Spiritual Laws* at Fort Totten Metro Train Station. It is a good place. People were very receptive.

Friday, August 7, 1992

I shared the *Four Spiritual Laws* with a man from Gambia, Africa. He was a Catholic. We went through the *Four Spiritual Laws*, but he didn't want to pray.

I started to share with a woman who was really friendly and eager. She was waiting for her girlfriend, who came around the second or third law, and we didn't finish.

I shared with a woman from Liberia who was a Christian. Two of her children were still in Liberia, and she would like to bring them to the United States so they could be with her. I promised to pray for her.

Monday, August 10, 1992

I shared the *Four Spiritual Laws* with a lady from the Philippines. She was Catholic and prayed with me to receive Jesus.

I gave a Gift to a man from the Middle East. He asked if it was okay since he wasn't a Christian. I said yes and briefly talked with him. He attended American University School of Internet Management.

I offered a Gift to a man who said, "No," and that it would make him throw up.

Another man used to be a Christian but had converted to Judaism. He believed they stole Jesus's body away from the tomb. He came from a good Christian family.

Tuesday, August 12, 1992

I shared the *Four Spiritual Laws* with a young lady who was a Christian and carried a Bible with her in her purse. We got to law 3, and her bus came.

I offered a post office clerk a Gift, and he said no.

I gave a Gift to a woman who had just arrived from Gambia, Africa. She didn't speak English very well and seemed threatened, so I moved on.

I offered a Gospel of John (Bread of Life version) to a retired army man who said he didn't eat bread, so he didn't take it. About five minutes later, he asked me if I worked in computers. We had a long talk. He was looking for an entry-level programmer position. I suggested he go to a community college and get some knowledge and experience. I shared how hard it is to break into the industry without experience. As I left, he took the Gospel of John.

Thursday, August 14, 1992

A lot of homeless people today. Two women. Both refused the Gift. One said she had had some bread earlier with butter. Lots of comedians lately. She seemed totally unreal. She had a magazine from which she showed pictures and talked about them.

The other lady who panhandled said there were a lot of homeless.

A homeless man with a bad rash accepted Jesus. He is the one who usually sleeps on one of the bus benches. He was pretty well dressed.

Wednesday, August 19, 1992

I shared the *Four Spiritual Laws* with a man who prayed the prayer and received Jesus as his Lord and Savior.

I shared with a college student who was with the Church

of Christ. He played the guitar. He didn't want a copy of the Gospel of John. He had his own Bible.

Thursday, August 20, 1992

I gave away Gifts at Catholic University Metro Train Station. I gave a Gift to a man who took it, said thanks, and walked away. He had been standing around for a while.

I gave a Gift to an Asian woman who said she was not religious. Her parents were Buddhists. She said she was an atheist. I didn't know how to deal with this. I should have had my response worked out.

I met a woman who was a Christian. We discussed evil in the world but didn't come up with any answers.

I gave a Gift to a man visiting from Bangladesh.

I met a woman who needed a church, preferably Episcopal. She wanted to talk. I should have taken the time to share the *Four Spiritual Laws* with her but didn't. This was a lost opportunity. I prayed for her.

Lesson Learned #42

At some point, you will meet an atheist or an agnostic. Understand what they believe and why they believe what they do. Be prepared with what you will say to them to try to convince them that there is a God and that they need him. When you meet someone from a cult religion, do your best to convert them to Christianity. After your encounter, spend some time researching their religion to better understand from where they are coming. This will prepare you to witness to them (and the next atheist or agnostic you meet) about Jesus.

Friday, August 21, 1992

I gave a Gift to a Cuban man. He gave it right back. He believed in God but hated religion.

I shared with a man and his two-year-old son. They were headed to the beach. I gave him a Gift and a *Four Spiritual Laws* to read on the way.

I shared the *Four Spiritual Laws* with a man who prayed and received Jesus as his Lord and Savior. He was a freshman at Radcliffe in Virginia.

Monday, August 24, 1992

I met a man who was a waiter at La Fontana. He was a Catholic and was very surprised that I was one as well. He didn't take the Gift, but he shook my hand, and we agreed that we needed to tell others about Jesus.

I offered a copy of "Juan" and the *Four Spiritual Laws* to three Spanish ladies. Two accepted, and one said, "No!" After she looked at what the others got, she changed her mind and asked for one.

A young lady, an Episcopalian, took a Gift. Her fiancé was Catholic. She thought that he would not convert.

I met a man who needed bus fare. I gave him a bus token and a Gift. He hung around for a while, and we talked. Later, he gave the Gospel of John back to me.

Thursday, August 27, 1992

At lunchtime, I went to Farragut Square Metro Train Station and handed out a hundred Gifts. I discovered that a park bench at Farragut Square is a good place to sit and give out Gifts.

Friday, August 28, 1992

I shared with a man who seemed incoherent. I gave him a Gift.

I gave a Gift to a woman who was a spiritualist—a person who believes that the spirits of the dead can communicate with living people. She seemed aggravated, so I left her alone. I did ask her about sin, but she said that she didn't want to talk about it.

I spoke with a man from Africa. He was a Catholic but became a Pentecostal and had fallen away from the church since he arrived in America. He was thinking about going back to the Catholic church. I started to share the *Four Spiritual Laws* with him, but his bus came.

I spoke with a Catholic woman who attended various churches. She seemed leery of the *Four Spiritual Laws*, but I shared them anyway. Her bus came, and I invited her to St. Mary's.

Thursday, September 3, 1992

I shared the *Four Spiritual Laws* with a man from Ecuador. He prayed and received Jesus as his Lord and Savior. He will look for a church. He was reading a Spanish version of the *Watchtower* (a Jehovah's Witness publication). He gave it to me, and I tossed it. He had been here a year and needed a job.

I spoke with a man who was Catholic. I gave him a Gift. When I tried to share the *Four Spiritual Laws* with him, he didn't feel like talking anymore. I left him alone.

Friday, September 4, 1992

I gave away Gifts at Catholic University Metro Train Station and fifty *Four Spiritual Laws* at the Wheaton Metro Train Station.

I shared the *Four Spiritual Laws* with a man who accepted Jesus as his Lord and Savior.

I shared the *Four Spiritual Laws* with a young lady. She and her boyfriend were waiting for a friend. The friend came, and she took the *Four Spiritual Laws* with her.

I met a young man who was a firefighter. He went to Catholic school but now was an agnostic. He said he would read the Gospel of John I gave him. I told him there were many answers in it.

I shared the *Four Spiritual Laws* with a very vocal young man. We didn't get to law 2 before his bus came. He shared how all his life he had the forty-five-minute Mass, which did nothing for him, and then he went to a nondenominational church, where the service ran for two hours throughout which he was totally elated.

I gave away a hundred Gifts at the Catholic University Metro Train Station.

I prayed with a man who received Jesus as his Lord and Savior after going through the *Four Spiritual Laws*. He experienced tears of joy.

One man, I think he was a priest, asked me what organization I was from. I told him I was doing this on my own.

While waiting for the metro, I gave a Gift to a man who was a pastor (at least that was the impression I had). He said he had seventeen theological degrees. His church was Corinthians Baptist Church.

When I reached Wheaton Metro Train Station, I gave out one pack (fifty) of the *Four Spiritual Laws*.

Thursday, September 10, 1992

Three people said no when I offered them a Gift. One man, I think he was Jewish, said he wasn't the right person for me. He was wrong.

I shared the *Four Spiritual Laws* with a man from South America. He was a Baptist. He attended church three to four times a week in his country, but while he attended church here, he wasn't as involved. He read along as I prayed, and he accepted Jesus as his Lord and Savior.

Tuesday, September 22, 1992

I met a homeless person from the Virgin Islands. I offered to buy him a hamburger, but he ordered chicken. He said he was from the tribe of Zebulon. He said the government had put out a contract on his life because he was a threat to President Reagan. His pinkie finger was swollen and bleeding. He said the police accused him of stealing, he fought with them, and they bit his finger. He believed in the Lord Jesus Christ.

I spoke with a Quaker. We talked about the Quaker church. He invited me to a meeting. I gave him a Gift.

I gave a woman a Gift and a *Four Spiritual Laws*. She prayed and received Jesus as her Lord and Savior.

Thursday, September 24, 1992

I gave out a hundred Gifts at the Silver Spring Metro Train Station. One woman asked me what church I was from. When I told her the Catholic church, she told me the priests molesting little boys should be punished and not sent back to a parish. I agreed with her.

There was a well-dressed man with a friend who first refused the Gift I offered him. Later, he came back and asked me for a Gospel of John and then again came back and asked for another copy for his friend.

Thursday, October 1, 1992

I gave out a hundred Gifts at Rhode Island Metro Train Station.

I met a Muslim, and we discussed the differences between

our religions. He was stumped by the difference between Jesus and other leaders and his claim and why he was crucified. Apparently, once you make it to Mecca, you are pure and holy, and your sins are forgiven.

Monday, October 5, 1992

I shared the *Four Spiritual Laws* with a man from Nicaragua. He prayed the Spanish version and received Jesus as his Lord and Savior.

Tuesday, October 6, 1992

I began to share the *Four Spiritual Laws* with a Baptist until his ride came (after law 3). He seemed very distracted.

Friday, October 9, 1992

I gave away Gifts at the Silver Spring Metro Train Station and twenty-five *Four Spiritual Laws* at the Wheaton Metro Train Station.

I shared the *Four Spiritual Laws* with a Christian man. He prayed and received Jesus as his Lord and Savior.

I shared the *Four Spiritual Laws* with another man who also was already a Christian. He didn't pray the prayer.

Tuesday, October 13, 1992

I gave away six Gifts. The first man said he would read it and let me know what he thought.

The second was a man from Indonesia. He was very pleasant but didn't take the Gift because of the language problem.

The third was a woman with whom I started to share the *Four Spiritual Laws*, but her bus came.

The fourth was an Englishman who was very impressed with what I was doing. He said he would talk to me after he read the Gospel of John.

The fifth was a young upcoming professional. He said he was a Christian but didn't go to church. He affirmed his Christianity numerous times while I was sharing the *Four Spiritual Laws* with him.

The sixth was a woman from Pennsylvania.

Wednesday, October 14, 1992

I gave a Gift and *Four Spiritual Laws* to a man who was waiting for a ride. He prayed with me and received Jesus as his Lord and Savior.

I began to share with a large man. I was just getting started with the *Four Spiritual Laws* when a lady friend arrived. I waited while he talked to her, and then he had to leave. I gave them both a Gift and a *Four Spiritual Laws* booklet.

Thursday, October 15, 1992

I gave away a hundred Gifts at Metro Center Train Station. I gave my last Gospel of John to a man and shared the *Four Spiritual Laws* with him. He prayed and received Jesus as his Lord and Savior.

Friday, October 16, 1992

I shared the *Four Spiritual Laws* with a man who received Jesus as his Lord and Savior. He prayed the prayer silently. He had lots of questions.

I met a young lady (early twenties) who had spent the night with a friend at Arlington Towers, and her car was towed away. She was trying to get money (twenty-five dollars), so she could get her car back. I offered to take her up there and pay (loan) her the money, but she wouldn't accept it from me because I was a "religious" man. I offered again, and she said she would think about it. I told her I would be leaving in a few minutes. She never came back to me.

Monday, October 19, 1992

I had lunch with John, who wants me to come to work at his company. We discussed a job offer, which I am seriously considering. It is a great opportunity professionally but a big decision because I would no longer be able to minister at the Rosslyn Metro Train Station during my lunch hour.

Wednesday, October 21, 1992

I prayed with a man today. I don't remember his name. He received Jesus as his Lord and Savior.

Thursday, October 22, 1992

I gave away Gifts and *Four Spiritual Laws* at the Catholic University Metro Train Station.

I prayed with a man who received Jesus as his Lord and Savior. We discussed the differences between Islam and Christianity.

Friday, October 23, 1992

I prayed with a man who received Jesus as his Lord and Savior.

I met one agnostic/atheist. She took a Gift but didn't want

to talk. When I asked her which she was, agnostic or atheist, she said she didn't think much about it.

I gave a Gift to Seek, a young lady from North India. She attended Georgetown. We had a nice conversation.

A man whom I have seen passing out Hyatt sale watch flyers began to talk to me. He was a Christian. I think he will be back next week to talk more.

Thursday, October 29, 1992

I gave out a hundred Gifts at McPherson Square Metro Train Station. It was very slow. It took about fifteen minutes.

Monday, November 2, 1992

I shared the *Four Spiritual Laws* and prayed with a woman who received Jesus as her Lord and Savior. She was going for a job physical tomorrow. If she passes, she will get the job. Her two kids are in a foster home. She will be able to get them back if she gets a job. Right now, she gets to see them once a week.

I met a Spanish guy from St. Charles Catholic Church. He talked a lot, especially about family values.

I was sharing with a salesman. He said he was familiar with the *Four Spiritual Laws*. As I began to share them with him, a man came up and asked for two copies of the Gospel of John. While I was dealing with him, the salesman left.

I gave a Gift to a pilot who was on his way back to England.

Thursday, November 5, 1992

I shared a Gift with a man from the Middle East. He was a PhD candidate at GW, or Georgetown. We first discussed the presidential campaign. I started to share the *Four Spiritual Laws* with him, but his bus came.

I shared a Gift and the *Four Spiritual Laws* with a man who was already a Christian, so he didn't pray with me. He had a new job that kept him from Bible study and church and was beginning to backslide. He was looking for a new job. I said I would pray for him. I suggested he look in the *Shepherd's Guide*.

Friday, November 6, 1992

I shared a Gift with a Methodist woman. I also gave her a *Four Spiritual Laws* when her ride came.

I had a debate with a man who believed in a universal religion. We debated whether or not Jesus was God. He sounded like he might be Muslim. We departed friends.

I shared a Gift and *Four Spiritual Laws* with a Methodist. He read silently as I read the prayer aloud. He said it was the desire of his heart and thanked me for spending the time with him.

On the way home, I stopped at a metro train station (I don't remember which one) and gave away 108 Gifts and 100 *Four Spiritual Laws*. There were many rejections.

One lady said, "What's this? The election is over."

Monday, November 9, 1992

I spent some time sharing with a young lady who worked for the Peace Corps. She became a Christian in 1975. She asked if I had received Jesus as my Lord and Savior. I shared about Bus Stop Ministry.

I spent some time with an elderly woman living in a shelter. She had had a tough life. I mostly listened.

Tuesday, November 10, 1992

I shared a Gift and *Four Spiritual Laws* with a young man. We prayed, and he received Jesus as his Lord and Savior.

Thursday, November 12, 1992

I started to share the *Four Spiritual Laws* with a man who was Catholic, but his bus came. He seemed to be listening, but his eyes were far away. He might have been under the influence of something.

Friday, November 13, 1992

There wasn't much activity today. I met a lady on the way over to the Rosslyn Metro Train Station. I gave her a Gift. She was a Christian and went to Nineteenth Street Baptist Church.

I gave a Gift to a person handing out flyers and one to a Spanish lady who spoke no English.

Wednesday, November 18, 1992

I shared the *Four Spiritual Laws* with two ladies—one who said she was a Christian and a young Catholic lady. Both ladies prayed the prayer of salvation with me.

Friday, November 20, 1992

I only had a short time at lunch today but was able to share the *Four Spiritual Laws* with two women. They both prayed with me to receive Jesus as their Lord and Savior.

On the way home, I stopped at the Takoma Park Metro Train Station. Not much happened. I gave out a hundred

Gifts, but the people were not very receptive. I do, however, believe that God answers my prayer that I pray each time I hand out Gifts: that each person who received a Gospel of John will come to know Jesus as Lord and Savior.

I was hoping to run into a man from the Witness Lee Church to discuss with him balance, love, and headship, but I didn't see him.

A man from the Christ Adelphian Church gave me a hand. He also gave me his phone number.

Monday, November 23, 1992

Today was a warm spring day. I shared a Gift and the *Four Spiritual Laws* with a woman who was a Christian but didn't have a church. She was looking for one. I read the prayer, and she agreed that it was the intention of her heart.

Monday, November 30, 1992

I shared a Gift and the *Four Spiritual Laws* with a man who came from a religious family but claimed to be an agnostic and didn't want to pray with me.

I shared a Gift and the *Four Spiritual Laws* with a man who prayed the prayer with me. He was from Bangladesh. He was here with his family looking for work.

Wednesday, December 2, 1992

I spent most of my lunch hour with a young man who used to belong to a church where he actively participated in Bible study and so on but hadn't attended in years. We just talked, and I encouraged him to find another church and attend. I also encouraged him to spend some time each day in prayer and Bible reading. I think he will. Our discussion seemed very productive.

Friday, December 4, 1992

I gave out 108 Gifts at the Wheaton Metro. I met a sixty-two-year-old Catholic woman (she looked to be in her twenties). She worked at one of the hotels in the area as a supervisor of cleaning (seven days a week). She went to Mass each morning. I gave her a Gift, and when I asked if she knew the Bible, she quoted John 3:16, but she said "forgotten son" rather than "begotten son."

After work, I stopped off at the Wheaton Metro Train Station on the way home. I was going to hand Gifts out at the Kiss and Ride, but I decided to go to the other end. When I got there, there were two young ladies and a man passing out advertising for tarot card reading. I gave them a Gift, and I prayed and tried to counter the tarot card advertisement by giving a Gift to each person who got the advertisement. One of the young ladies stopped handing out the advertising and began to read the Gospel of John.

The man was their father. He came over to me and asked, "Mary?" I am not sure what he meant. He was new in the area, from Dallas. He was Catholic and concerned that he had to leave the Catholic church to become a Christian as some friends had told him. I told him I was Catholic, and he seemed surprised. He asked me more questions. I told him I went to St. Mary's Catholic Church and where it was. I also told him that St. John the Evangelist Catholic Church was just down the road. He said that going to church was important. Then I asked if he had ever heard of the *Four Spiritual Laws*. He said no, so I shared the *Four Spiritual Laws* with him. He prayed the prayer to receive Jesus Christ as his Lord and Savior. He said he would look for me again. After he left, it occurred to me that I should have asked for his phone number. Then it occurred to me that it was on the tarot card advertisement.

Monday, December 7, 1992

I gave my two weeks' notice at work and would be leaving to join the new company. This would mean the end to my lunch-hour Bus Stop Ministry. I was sad about this but decided that I could still stop at metro stations on the way to work and the way home and pass out Gifts and *Four Spiritual Laws* booklets. Somehow, I would try to continue the one-on-one but wasn't sure how.

I got out late to the Rosslyn Metro Train Station. Two new vendors were there. I gave a Gift and a *Four Spiritual Laws* to a man who prayed and received Jesus. He had been in the area for the last four years. He hadn't found a church yet. I encouraged him to find one.

I started to share the *Four Spiritual Laws* with a vendor from Afghanistan. Just about got to step 4 and a "Christian" woman came to ask for her money back for a watch she had purchased from the vendor. She said to me, "Is this the kind of man you want to witness to?" She was really mad. I had to leave. When I looked back, the police were there.

I called the tarot card man. Some woman answered and sounded really nasty. She wanted to know who I was and how I had met him. She said she would let him know I called. He never called me back.

Tuesday, December 8, 1992

I met a young Haitian man, and I shared the *Four Spiritual Laws* with him. He prayed and asked Jesus to be his Lord and Savior.

Wednesday, December 9, 1992

I had dinner at my father-in-law's. I shared the *Four Spiritual Laws* with him. He prayed and invited Jesus into his life as his Lord and Savior.

Thursday, December 10, 1992

It snowed today. I ate at Roy's. I helped an elderly lady across the sky walk and gave her a Gift. I was sure she was going to slip.

Friday, December 11, 1992

I gave away Gifts at Wheaton Metro Train Station. I shared the *Four Spiritual Laws* with two people who both prayed and received Jesus.

Monday, December 14 to Friday, December 18, Vacation

Monday, December 21, 1992

I gave out Gifts at the Wheaton Metro Train Station in the morning.

I met a man who once belonged to Riverdale Baptist Church but had been away for about a year. He was thinking about returning. I told him about my friend who attended there and encouraged him to return. He was impressed by my commitment to sharing the Gospel, and I was encouraged.

I had a farewell lunch with the programming staff today.

Tuesday, December 22, 1992

I gave out Gifts at the Rockville Metro Train Station.
I had a farewell lunch with my friend Lyndon today.

Wednesday, December 23, 1992

I gave away Gifts at Rhode Island Metro Train Station.

Today was the Data Systems Christmas luncheon.

At the Rhode Island Metro Train Station, the people were really receptive. Four or five asked for extra copies to give to others. I only found one Gospel of John in the trash can—very unusual.

I shared the *Four Spiritual Laws* with Lois today after I gave her my Christmas gift. She prayed with me and received Jesus as her Lord and Savior.

CHAPTER 11

Conclusion

> Christ has no body now on earth but yours; no
> hands but yours; no feet but yours. Yours are
> the eyes through which Christ's compassion is
> to look out to the world. Yours are the feet with
> which he is to go about doing good. Yours are
> the hand with which he is to bless now.
>
> —St. Teresa of Avila

We have freely received; we are to freely give. I discovered that it is an adventure each time you share the Good News with someone. Each person is different, and witnessing requires waiting upon the Lord, listening to his voice, and following the lead of the Holy Spirit. The work is challenging, but the rewards are out of this world.

At the end of 1992, I started a new job, which ended my lunch-hour visits at the Rosslyn Metro Train Station. Taking the new job required me to leave the Rosslyn area. During my time spent in Rosslyn, I learned a lot about witnessing and had the wonderful opportunity to share Jesus. All in all, in the two years in Rosslyn, I gave away over eight thousand Gospel of John booklets and over three thousand of the *Four Spiritual Laws* booklets. I learned many lessons (see Appendix A for a complete list of them) about witnessing, but the most exciting and gratifying aspect of it all was the time that I spent with total strangers telling them about Jesus. Every day was an adventure. Some of them prayed with me and received Jesus as their personal Lord and Savior. That was particularly rewarding. My experience of receiving Jesus as my Lord and Savior was the single most wonderful experience in my life, and it was such a blessing to help others experience what I had when they prayed with me to receive Jesus. This brought great joy to me, and I know that the angels in heaven were rejoicing over them. My only regret was that I couldn't go with them as they moved on to the next step of getting involved with a church and growing in Christ.

I knew that at my new job I wouldn't have the same opportunity to sit at the bus station on my lunch hour and wait for someone to sit next to me so I could offer him or her a Gift, but I still wanted to share the Good News. I ended up driving to a different Metro station after work once a week. I wasn't able to go every week but went as often as I could and ended up going most weeks. Each visit I made it a point to give a hundred Gifts. Think about that. One half hour a week, that's all it takes. As I passed out the Gifts and as the Spirit led me, I looked for opportunities to share the *Four Spiritual Laws* and to lead someone to the Lord.

I was convinced that each person I approached was, in a way, a divine appointment. I was available to share the Good News with anyone who would listen, and God faithfully brought them to me so I could. Not everyone accepted Jesus, but I felt that as each left with the Gift I had given him or her and my prayer for his or her salvation, that that person was that much closer to coming to the Lord. Some plant, some water, but God gives the growth. I also envisioned that those who went away with their Gospel of John might end up sharing it with someone else.

My purpose in writing this book was to tell my story about how God filled me with an overflowing desire to witness to others by telling them about Jesus. As a new Christian, I wanted others to experience Jesus as I did, but I didn't know how to make that happen. At first, I stumbled quite a bit, but with God's help, I was able to work out the kinks and learned how to do it. My hope is that my experience will be helpful to others who want to witness, but be assured, if you have the desire, God can use you, and he will direct and guide you along the way. "The harvest is plentiful, but the laborers are few" (Matthew 9:37), and God is looking for willing workers. The pay isn't much, but the rewards are great.

While you are not in it for the glory, God will richly bless you as you encounter the unsaved and do your part to help them to find Jesus. My prayer for you is that God will richly bless you and enable you to go out and share his love with all you meet.

My email address is pete@whitfords.org. Please don't hesitate to contact me if you have any comments or questions or if I can help you in any way to go out and share the Good News of Jesus Christ.

God bless you!

Peter D. Whitford

APPENDIX A

Lessons Learned

Lesson Learned #1: If you want to share the Good News of Jesus Christ, you need to first prepare. This preparation consists of developing the following:

- Approach—how will you approach the person to whom you are going to witness?
- Present—how can you quickly and efficiently share the Good News? (What are you going to say, and how are you going to say it?)
- Ask—after presenting the Gospel, how will you ask them if they would like to make a commitment to receive Jesus Christ as their Lord and Savior?
- Pray for those who say yes—What prayer will you use? Prepare one in advance and memorize it.
- For those who say no, leave the door open. Give them a *Four Spiritual Laws* booklet to take away with them and hope they will read and think about it.

- For those who receive Jesus, share the four things to focus on from chapter 4.
- Close—this will be different for those who accept Jesus and those who don't.

Lesson Learned #2: Practice, practice, practice your presentation.

Lesson Learned #3: There will be rejection. Some people will refuse a Gift because they don't know what it is and don't want to be bothered. Others may know what is and reject it. In this case, realize that they are not rejecting you, but they are rejecting God (see Luke 10:16).

Lesson Learned #4: Some people that you witness to will disagree, even argue with you. Be kind and understanding. Listen to what they are saying. You don't have to agree with them, but be kind and gentle. Scripture reminds us we are to

- "Always be prepared to make a defense to any one who calls you to account for the hope that is in you, yet do it with gentleness and reverence" (1 Peter 3:15).
- "Let your speech always be gracious, seasoned with salt, so that you may know how you ought to answer every one" (Colossians 4:6).

Remember that your goal is not to win arguments but to win souls to Jesus. Even though you know you could win the argument, don't. If you win the argument, you may lose the soul that you are trying to save.

Lesson Learned #5: When I was witnessing on a daily basis, there were some days when nothing appeared to happen (dry spell). Even though I didn't see anything happening, I needed to be assured that God was working. My job was to hand out the Gospel of John. God is using me for that purpose. Sometimes during a dry spell, I was all of sudden surprised by God. God caused something to happen when I least expected it, and as a result, I was richly blessed. Being surprised by God is not only amazing, but his surprises were confirmations that I was doing what I was supposed to be doing.

Lesson Learned #6: It occurred to me that when I was sharing Jesus with someone, it could just be a random encounter, or it could be a divine appointment. God wants everyone to have everlasting life. He works in the lives of the unsaved and provides them with the opportunity to receive Jesus. To do this, there has to be someone who is willing to tell them about Jesus. God knows when a person is ready to accept Christ, and he provides the circumstances for the encounter to take place. In any case, I knew that when I approached people and gave them a Gift, I might never know the fruit that that encounter might bear, but I knew that the person I gave it to would be closer to God as a result of it. God is looking for faithful servants who will share the Good News, and when he finds one, he will work out the details providing the opportunities for that person to witness. Remember, some plant, some water, but God gives the growth.

Lesson Learned #7: The Multiplication Effect — Some who received the Gift would share it with friends and family because they just thought it was a nice gift or because they thought the person they shared it with needed to hear the message.

Lesson Learned #8: At the Wonder Bread store, I was given the opportunity to share my faith with someone who just happened to be of the same faith community as me. Throughout this ministry, I had the opportunity to share with people of many other faith backgrounds—Baptists, Evangelicals, Mormons, Jehovah's Witnesses, those of the Jewish and Islamic faiths, and others. I took an interest in learning what others believed, and then, when given the opportunity, I used that knowledge to share the Good News with them. It became easier as time went on, and as my knowledge increased, I became better prepared and more proficient at sharing the Good News.

Lesson Learned #9: I discovered that when you openly share your faith with others, they often will open up about theirs. Sometimes they even share that they don't have any faith and why.

Lesson Learned #10: I came to the conclusion that when people say no or refuse the Gift, it isn't necessarily because it is a Christian Bible book. For the most part, when I approach people offering them a free Gift, they have no idea what it is. A lot of people subscribe to the adage that there is no such thing as a free lunch (gift), and there is always a catch, requiring something from you that makes the free gift not so free. I could have been a salesman selling timeshares for all they knew. In any case, I concluded that I shouldn't think that they were rejecting the Gift but that they just didn't believe that it was really free and didn't want to be bothered.

Lesson Learned #11: I observed that when there was a group, people were less likely to accept the Gift because of the presence of the others. They also might react in a negative or smart-alecky manner, so it would be better to avoid groups.

Lesson Learned #12: You will encounter people that have deep seeded problems which will be beyond your scope to deal with and solve. Develop a list of pastors, social workers and others that are trained to handle these kinds of issues. Then when you encounter someone who needs help, you can refer them to an appropriate resource.

Lesson Learned #13: Keep your ears open and listen to what people say to you. Most won't come up and ask you to tell them about the Good News. They will come back with questions or comments that you need to be able to interpret and use as a lead-in to the Good News message.

Lesson Learned #14: I noticed that if the first person in a queue heading for or exiting out of the metro said no when I offered the Gift, then the rest of the people in the group would most likely say no. If the first one of a group took the Gift, then the rest of the group would most likely take the Gift as well. They didn't want to miss out on the free something that the person before them received.

Lesson Learned #15: It is essential to have a Bible with you in a ministry like this. People will ask you questions that can only be answered from scripture. The best way to answer their questions is to open up the Bible to the relevant chapter and verse and then let them read it. Also, if you don't know the answer or the scripture location, tell them that and that you will research it and get back to them. Try to set up a time and place to meet.

Lesson Learned #16: When people say that they are already Christians and that I should give the Gift to someone else, it creates a great opportunity to offer the option for them to give it to someone else. I can say something like, "You are a Christian—great! Do you know someone who isn't a Christian and might benefit from it?" Take the opportunity to encourage others to reach out to the unsaved they know. This gives them a great way to witness to them. All Christians are called to witness, but some find it hard to do. This challenge gives them an opportunity.

Lesson Learned #17: When meeting people of other faiths and denominations, the best approach is to just share my Christian faith and to follow the leading of the Holy Spirit.

Lesson Learned #18: The best approach to dealing with metro employees is to respect them and do what they say. They are only doing their job. Each employee is different. Some don't really care whether you distribute information, and others don't seem to want you to do it. For the latter, I don't know if it is because they don't like what you are distributing or if it is because metro has some sort of policy regarding distribution. In any case, I made a conscious decision not to be confrontational with them.

Lesson Learned #19: Opportunities to share one-on-one happen very quickly, and you have to be ready when the opportunity arises.

Lesson Learned #20: I seem to be facing more situations where people open up to me with their issues and problems. I see this as a great opportunity to pray with them. It takes some courage to offer prayer to someone you don't know and have just met, but it can be very rewarding for all those who say yes. If people don't feel comfortable praying with a stranger, that is okay too. It's really up to them and how the Holy Spirit is working in their life.

Lesson Learned #21: There is a great temptation to keep in contact with some I meet. I don't think it is prudent to give out my phone number to a total stranger, but it might be okay to give out my email. An even better idea would be to set up a special email for Bus Stop Ministry. If people really want to stay in contact, then have them give you their phone or email.

Lesson Learned #22: After a few months, I began to see and offer Gifts to the same people. Even though I went to different metro stations, if I got there at about the same time I had been there before, chances were that I would see some of the same people. There is really no way to remember them all, but if they indicate that they already have received a Gift, then it is a great opportunity to get them into a conversation by asking if they read it or what they thought of it.

Those who have already said no may seem annoyed. However, if they say anything, it gives me a chance to discuss it with them. The key is to listen closely to the Holy Spirit and allow him to guide you.

Lesson Learned #23: I am much more comfortable now with giving Gifts to people who work where I do than I was before. At first, I was worried about what they might think. Now it doesn't really matter to me. In my experience, coworkers are a bit more receptive than most. When they notice me, they usually approach me. Also, it sets up an opportunity for me. If they ever have any questions or want to talk, they now know they can find me.

Lesson Learned #24: It's impossible to know what people do with the Gifts I give them. They may trash them, put them away, or—I hope—read them. If they do read them, what will they do next? Again, it is not for me to know.

My grandmother gave me copies of the Gospel of John. I just put them in my dresser drawer. I looked at them from time to time, and I truly believe that the message I found there had a large part in my conversion to Christianity.

I continue to pray that all who receive the Gifts will read them and come to know Jesus, but that is up to them. I continue to pray and believe that the Holy Spirit is working in each of them and that simply by my handing them out, whether they read or toss them, God is using me as his instrument to spread the Good News. Remember that *"Paul planted, Apollos watered, but God gave the growth. So neither he who plants nor he who waters will see anything, but only God who gives the growth"* (1 Corinthians 3:6–7).

Lesson Learned #25: When people share their faith with you, pause and take the time to let them tell their story. Get to know them. Make as many friends in Christ as you can. Establishing a relationship with them may provide an opportunity to pray for their needs or have them pray for yours.

Lesson Learned #26: Observation: since the beginning of Bus Stop Ministry, it seems that mostly blue-collar workers and minorities are interested in what I am offering. Young, upscale professionals seem to reject my offering. I don't even think that most of them know what I am offering, they just reject it. I am not sure what this means. It is just something I have observed.

Lesson Learned #27: The young lady who was going to sell my Gifts back to me made me realize something that I suspected: many people are being offered or receiving multiple Gifts. This may explain some rejections—they already have one. It made me wonder which person I had given the most.

To somewhat compensate for this, I began visiting different metro stations and tried to change the time I visited a station by ten or fifteen minutes. It makes sense that many people leave work at the same time each day and arrive at the metro station at the same time, give or take a few minutes. But since there are so many people who enter each station between four and seven in the evening, I can work it out so I won't see the same people all the time.

Lesson Learned #28: It is becoming clearer and clearer to me that people waiting for a bus don't seem to mind talking while they wait for their bus. It's a great opportunity to share Jesus with them.

Lesson Learned #29: No fruit without roots. When I first started witnessing, I was nervous and worried about what people would think (of me), but I didn't give up. I persevered, and after a while, I began to produce fruits. As scripture says, "Blessed is the man who trusts in the Lord, whose trust is the Lord. He is like a tree planted by water, that sends out its roots by the stream, and does not fear when heat comes, for its leaves remain green, and is not anxious in the year of drought, for it does not cease to bear fruit" (Jeremiah 17:7–8).

In the beginning, I lacked confidence and was somewhat awkward in my presentation. I suspect people noticed this, but I trusted in the Lord, and once I established my roots, I began to produce fruit. As I grew more confident, people were more willing to listen and respond.

Lesson Learned #30: Whenever people seem interested and want to talk, I should stop what I am doing, focus on them, and follow the lead of the Holy Spirit. This is what I want to do with all that the Lord brings to me. My problem is that sometimes I don't recognize it right away, and I stand a chance of the person wandering off.

Lesson Learned #31: One disadvantage of evangelizing at a bus stop is that you may be in the middle of sharing with a person and the bus comes. If you are using the *Four Spiritual Laws*, then it is best to give it to the person and ask them to finish reading it. This might be a good opportunity to leave a phone number or an email in case they want to talk or have any questions. You could ask them to let you know what they think.

Lesson Learned #32: Apologetics contains a large number of issues, but each of them is important. Some important rules for being an apologist are:

- Study, study, and study issues in your spare time.
- Be accepting of the other person but not necessarily his or her point of view.
- If you don't know the answer to a question, say you don't know and that you will research it and get back to the person (try for an appointment).

- If you are going to use a scripture, know the book, chapter, and verse. Otherwise, don't use it.
- Be polite. You don't just want to win the battle and lose the war.

Lesson Learned #33: It is really important to smile. People seem to be more receptive and open when you do. I guess when you look too serious, people must suspect you are up to no good.

Lesson Learned #34: When facing someone who is angry or violent, keep the following tips in mind.

- Pray for help.
- Don't strike back.
- Avoid the person if possible.
- Move away from him or her.

Lesson Learned #35: I must be very careful not to judge. I can usually tell whether a person will accept a tract, but I want to be sure, so I offer one to everyone regardless. Sometimes I am surprised when someone I thought wouldn't be interested takes one.

Lesson Learned #36: People don't always know what I am offering and may reject my offer just because they don't want to be bothered and not necessarily because they are not interested.

Lesson Learned #37: Sharing the gospel with a group creates a different dynamic than sharing with one person. People are less open when others are around. They don't know what others think and accordingly may be less open to accepting what they are hearing.

Lesson Learned #38: I find that when I show I am sincerely interested in the people I meet, they are more receptive when I share the Gift or *Four Spiritual Laws* with them. It only takes a second or two to observe a person and find something unique about him or her.

Lesson Learned #39: I must not look on the outward person but realize the inward person is the real one and the one seeking God. Just like scripture says in 1 Samuel 16:7, "But the Lord said to Samuel, 'Do not look on his appearance or on the height of his stature, because I have rejected him; for the Lord sees not as man sees; man looks on the outward appearance, but the Lord looks on the heart.'"

Lesson Learned #40: When the Spirit uses you to share the Good News with someone, you should do just that regardless of your mood or how you feel. You will be pleasantly surprised with the fruit of your sharing. You just don't know what the person may be thinking, and you don't know how God is working in his or her life. Your feelings or mood may be a result of an attack by the evil one, who of course doesn't want you to succeed.

Lesson Learned #41: Take the time to talk with people after praying with them for salvation. Try to find out more about them and what their needs are. Pray with them for their needs.

Lesson Learned #42: At some point, you will meet an atheist or an agnostic. Understand what they believe and why they believe what they do. Be prepared with what you will say to them to convince them that there is a God and that they need him. When you meet someone from a cult religion, do your best to convert them to Christianity. After your encounter, spend some time researching their religion to better understand from where they are coming. This will prepare you to witness to them (and the next atheist, agnostic, or cult member you meet) about Jesus.

APPENDIX B

Tract Count

Date	Location	GOJ	Total GOJ	Annual Total	Four Laws	Total Laws	Annual Total
12/20/90	Work—Gifts	6					
12/27/90	Shopping Center	12					
12/28/90	Wonder Bread Store	2					
	Total Dec. 1990		20				
	Total 1990			20			
1/2/91	Wheaton	12					
1/3/91	On the way to work	12					
1/4/91	Rosslyn	12					
1/7/91	Rosslyn	12					
1/8/91	Rosslyn	8					
1/10/91	Rosslyn	12					
1/19/91	Bob's Big Boy	24					
1/22/91	Rosslyn	12					
1/23/91	Rosslyn	12					

Date	Location	*GOJ*	Total *GOJ*	Annual Total	*Four Laws*	Total *Laws*	Annual Total
1/24/12	Rosslyn	12					
1/29/91	Rosslyn	12					
1/30/91	Rosslyn	12					
1/31/91	Rosslyn	12					
	Total Jan. 1991		164				
2/1/91	Rosslyn	12					
2/4/91	Rosslyn	12					
2/5/91	Rosslyn	24					
2/6/91	Rosslyn	24					
2/7/91	Rosslyn	18					
2/8/91	Rosslyn	18					
2/11/91	Rosslyn	18					
2/12/91	Rosslyn	18					
2/13/91	Rosslyn	18					
2/14/91	Rosslyn	18					
2/15/91	Rosslyn	18					
2/19/91	Rosslyn	18					
2/20/91	Rosslyn	18					
2/21/18	Rosslyn	18					
2/22/91	Rosslyn	24					
2/25/91	Rosslyn	18					
2/26/91	Rosslyn	18					
2/27/91	Rosslyn	18					
2/28/91	Rosslyn	18					
	Total Feb. 1991		348				
3/1/91	Rosslyn	24					
3/5/91	Rosslyn	18					
3/6/18	Rosslyn	18					
3/11/91	Rosslyn	18					
3/12/91	Rosslyn	18					
3/13/91	Rosslyn	18					

Date	Location	GOJ	Total GOJ	Annual Total	Four Laws	Total Laws	Annual Total
3/14/91	Rosslyn	18					
3/15/91	Rosslyn	18					
3/18/91	Rosslyn	18					
3/20/91	Rosslyn	18					
3/21/91	Rosslyn	18					
3/22/91	Rosslyn	24					
3/25/91	Rosslyn	18					
3/26/91	Rosslyn	18					
3/28/91	Rosslyn	18					
3/30/91	Rosslyn	36					
	Total Mar. 1991		318				
4/1/91	Rosslyn	18					
4/2/91	Rosslyn	18					
4/3/91	Rosslyn	18					
4/4/91	Rosslyn	18					
4/5/91	Rosslyn	24					
4/8/91	Rosslyn	18					
4/9/91	Rosslyn	18					
4/10/91	Rosslyn	18					
4/11/91	Rosslyn	18					
4/12/91	Rosslyn	24					
4/15/91	Rosslyn	18					
4/16/91	Rosslyn	18					
4/17/91	Rosslyn	18					
4/18/91	Rosslyn	18					
4/19/91	Various Places	402			100		
4/22/91	Rosslyn	18					
4/23/91	Rosslyn	18					
4/24/91	Rosslyn	18					
4/25/91	Rosslyn	18					
4/26/91	Rosslyn	18					

Date	Location	GOJ	Total GOJ	Annual Total	*Four Laws*	Total *Laws*	Annual Total
4/29/91	Rosslyn	18					
4/30/91	Rosslyn	18					
	Total for Apr. 1991		792			100	
5/1/91	Rosslyn	18					
5/2/24	Rosslyn	24					
5/3/91	Rosslyn	18					
5/6/91	Rosslyn	18					
5/7/91	Rosslyn	18					
5/13/91	Rosslyn	18					
5/14/91	Rosslyn	18					
5/15/91	Rosslyn	18					
5/16/91	Rosslyn	18					
5/17/91	Gallery Place	24			95		
5/20/91	Rosslyn	18			50		
5/21/91	Rosslyn	18					
5/22/91	Rosslyn	18					
5/23/91	Rosslyn	18					
5/24/91	Foggy Bottom	6			50		
5/28/91	Rosslyn	18					
5/29/91	Rosslyn	18					
5/30/91	Rosslyn	18					
5/31/91	Clarendon				30		
	Total for May		324			225	
6/3/91	Rosslyn	18					
6/4/91	Rosslyn	18					
6/5/91	Rosslyn	18					
6/6/91	Rosslyn	18					
6/7/91	McPherson Square	18			50		
6/8/91	Federal Triangle						

Date	Location	GOJ	Total GOJ	Annual Total	*Four Laws*	Total *Laws*	Annual Total
6/10/91	Rosslyn	18					
6/11/91	Rosslyn	18					
6/12/91	Rosslyn	18					
6/13/91	Rosslyn	18			50		
6/14/91	Foggy Bottom	18			50		
6/17/91	Rosslyn	18					
6/18/91	Tenley	18			50		
6/25/91	Rosslyn	18					
6/26/91	Rosslyn	18					
6/27/91	Rosslyn	18					
6/28/91	Rosslyn	24					
	Total for June		294			200	
7/5/91	Rosslyn	24					
7/8/91	Rosslyn	18					
7/9/91	Rosslyn	18					
7/10/91	Rosslyn	18					
7/11/91	Rosslyn	18					
7/12/91	McPherson Square				65		
7/16/91	Rosslyn	18					
7/17/91	Rosslyn	18					
7/18/91	Rosslyn	18					
7/19/91	Silver Spring	24			100		
7/22/91	Rosslyn	18					
7/23/91	Rosslyn	18					
7/24/91	Rosslyn	18					
7/25/91	Rosslyn	18					
7/26/91	McPherson Square	24			100		
7/19/91	Rosslyn	18					
7/30/91	Rosslyn	18					
7/31/91	Rosslyn	18					

Date	Location	GOJ	Total GOJ	Annual Total	Four Laws	Total Laws	Annual Total
	Total for July		324			265	
8/1/91	Rosslyn	18					
8/2/91	Rosslyn	24					
8/5/91	Rosslyn	18					
8/6/91	Rosslyn	18					
8/8/91	Rosslyn	18					
8/9/91	Rosslyn	24					
8/12/91	Rosslyn	18					
8/13/91	Rosslyn	18					
8/15/21	Rosslyn	18					
8/16/91	Rosslyn	24					
8/19/91	Rosslyn	18					
8/20/91	Rosslyn	18					
8/21/91	Rosslyn	18					
8/22/91	Rosslyn	18					
8/23/91	Rockville	18			100		
8/26/91	Rosslyn	18					
8/27/91	Rosslyn	18					
8/28/91	Rosslyn	18					
8/29/91	Rosslyn	18					
8/30/91	Rosslyn	18					
	Total for August		378			100	
9/9/91	Rosslyn	18					
9/10/91	Rosslyn	18					
9/11/91	Rosslyn	18					
9/13/91	Metro Center	24			45		
9/16/91	Rosslyn	18					
9/17/91	Rosslyn	18					
9/18/91	Rosslyn	18					

Date	Location	GOJ	Total GOJ	Annual Total	*Four Laws*	Total *Laws*	Annual Total
9/19/91	Rosslyn	24					
9/20/91	Rosslyn	24					
9/23/91	Rosslyn	18					
9/26/91	Rosslyn	18					
	Total for Sept.		216			45	
10/10/91	Rosslyn	18					
10/11/91	Metro Center	24			50		
10/15/91	Rosslyn	18					
10/16/91	Rosslyn	18					
10/21/91	Metro Center				30		
10/22/91	Rosslyn	18					
10/23/91	Rosslyn	18					
10/24/91	Rosslyn	18					
10/25/91	Metro Center	24			50		
10/28/91	Rosslyn	18					
10/29/91	Rosslyn	18					
10/30/91	Rosslyn	18					
10/31/91	Rosslyn	18					
	Total for Oct.		228			130	
11/1/91	Metro Center	50					
11/5/91	Rosslyn	18					
11/6/91	Rosslyn	18					
11/7/91	Rockville				50		
11/8/91	Shady Grove	54			50		
11/12/91	Rosslyn	18					
11/13/91	Rosslyn	18					
11/14/91	Rosslyn	18					
11/15/91	Shady Grove	24			450		
11/18/91	Rosslyn	18					

Date	Location	GOJ	Total GOJ	Annual Total	Four Laws	Total Laws	Annual Total
11/19/91	Rosslyn	18					
11/20/91	Rosslyn						
11/21/91	Rosslyn	18					
11/22/91	Shady Grove	18			100		
11/25/91	Rosslyn	18					
11/26/91	Rosslyn	18					
11/27/91	Rosslyn	18					
	Total for Nov.		344			650	
12/2/91	Rosslyn	18					
12/3/91	Rosslyn	18					
12/4/91	Rosslyn	18					
12/5/91	Wheaton	18			50		
12/6/24	Metro Center	24					
12/13/91	Rockville	24			50		
12/16/91	Rosslyn	18					
12/17/91	Rosslyn	18					
12/18/91	Grosvenor	60					
12/19/91	Tenley	66					
12/20/91	Fort Totten	84					
12/23/91	Rockville	18			40		
12/24/91	Metro Center	84			200		
12/31/91	Metro Center				250		
	Total for Dec.		468			590	
	Total for 1991			4198			2305
1/2/92	Rosslyn	18					
1/3/91	Rosslyn	24					
1/6/92	Rockville	18			50		
1/7/92	Rosslyn	18					
1/8/92	Rosslyn	18					

Date	Location	GOJ	Total GOJ	Annual Total	Four Laws	Total Laws	Annual Total
1/10/92	Rosslyn	24					
1/13/92	Rosslyn	18					
1/14/92	Fort Totten				100		
1/16/92	Rosslyn	18					
1/17/92	Metro Center	24					
1/21/92	Grosvenor						
1/22/92	Rosslyn						
1/23/92	Rockville						
1/24/92	Rosslyn	24					
1/28/92	Rosslyn	18					
1/29/92	Rosslyn	18					
1/30/92	Rosslyn	18					
1/31/92	Rosslyn	18					
	Total for Jan.		276			150	
2/3/92	Rosslyn	18					
2/4/92	Rosslyn	18					
2/5/92	Rosslyn	18					
2/6/92	Rosslyn	18					
2/7/92	Rosslyn	24					
2/10/92	Rosslyn	18					
2/11/92	Rosslyn	18					
2/12/92	Rosslyn	12					
2/13/92	Rosslyn	18					
2/14/92	Rosslyn	24					
2/18/92	Rosslyn	18					
2/19/92	Rosslyn	18					
2/20/92	Rosslyn	18					
2/21/92	Metro Center	24			125		
2/24/92	Rosslyn	18					
2/25/92	Rosslyn	18					

Date	Location	GOJ	Total GOJ	Annual Total	Four Laws	Total Laws	Annual Total
2/26/92	Rosslyn	18					
2/28/92	Rosslyn	24			150		
	Total for Feb.		342			275	
3/2/92	Rosslyn	18					
3/3/92	Rosslyn	18					
3/4/92	Rosslyn	18					
3/5/92	Rosslyn	18					
3/6/92	Metro Center	24			150		
3/9/92	Rosslyn	18					
3/10/92	Rosslyn	18					
3/11/92	Rosslyn	18					
3/12/92	Rosslyn	18					
3/13/92	Rockville	18			100		
3/16/92	Tenley						
3/17/92	Rosslyn						
3/18/92	Rosslyn	18					
3/19/92	Rosslyn	18					
3/20/92	Rosslyn	24					
3/23/92	Rosslyn	24					
3/24/92	Rosslyn	18					
3/25/92	Rosslyn	18					
3/26/92	Rosslyn	18					
3/27/92	Rosslyn	24					
3/30/92	Rosslyn	24					
3/31/92	Rosslyn	24					
	Total for Mar.		396			250	
4/1/92	Rosslyn	18					
4/2/92	Rosslyn	18					
4/3/92	Rosslyn	24					

Date	Location	GOJ	Total GOJ	Annual Total	Four Laws	Total Laws	Annual Total
4/6/92	Rosslyn	18					
4/7/92	Rosslyn	18					
4/8/92	Rosslyn	18					
4/9/92	Rosslyn	18					
4/13/92	Rosslyn	24					
4/14/92	Rosslyn	18					
4/17/92	Metro Center	408					
4/30/92	Rockville	150					
	Total for Apr.		732				
5/14/92	Wheaton	150					
5/20/92	Rosslyn	18					
5/21/92	Rosslyn	18					
5/22/92	Rosslyn	24					
5/26/92	Rosslyn	18					
5/27/92	Rosslyn	18					
	Total for May		246				
6/2/92	Rosslyn	18					
6/12/92	Wheaton	100					
6/19/92	Farragut North/West	66					
	Total for June		184				
7/28/92	Metro Center	100					
7/31/92	Rhode Island	100					
	Total for July		200				
8/4/92	Fort Totten				50		
8/20/92	Catholic University	100					
8/27/92	Farragut Square	100					
	Total for Aug.		200			50	

Date	Location	GOJ	Total GOJ	Annual Total	Four Laws	Total Laws	Annual Total
9/4/92	CU / Wheaton	100			50		
9/24/17	Silver Spring	100					
	Total for September		200			50	
10/1/92	Rhode Island	100					
10/9/92	Silver Spring / Wheaton	120			25		
10/13/92	Rosslyn	6					
10/15/92	Metro Center	100					
10/20/92	Rosslyn	2			2		
10/22/92	Catholic University	108			100		
10/29/92	McPherson Square	100					
	Total for Oct.		536			127	
11/6/92	Don't Remember	108			100		
11/20/92	Takoma Park	100					
	Total for Nov.		208			100	
12/4/92	Wheaton	108					
12/11/92	Wheaton	108					
12/21/92	Wheaton	108					
12/22/92	Rockville	200					
12/23/92	Rhode Island	108					
	Total for Dec.		632			0	
				4,152			1,002
	Grand Total	8,370	8,370	8,370	3,307	3,307	3,307

ABOUT THE AUTHOR

In April of 1974, in a hotel in Rochester New York, the author had a personal encounter with the Lord Jesus Christ and experienced the peace which passes all understanding. It was such an amazing event that he wanted to go out and share it with others. Not only did he want to tell them what happened, but he wanted them to experience that same peace which passes all understanding that he had experienced.

The Author is a graduate of the University of Maryland, University College, where he studied computers and management information systems, and a graduate of Education Parish Services which is a four-year certificate program focusing on serving in the church.

Printed in the United States
By Bookmasters